Contexts in Literature

ll

rian Barlow

CAMBRIDGE
UNIVERSITY PRESS

CAMBRIDGE UNIVERSITY PRESS
Cambridge, New York, Melbourne, Madrid, Cape Town, Singapore,
São Paulo, Delhi

Cambridge University Press
The Edinburgh Building, Cambridge CB2 8RU, UK

www.cambridge.org
Information on this title: www.cambridge.org/9780521729826

First published 2009

Printed in the United Kingdom at the University Press, Cambridge

A catalogue record for this publication is available from the British Library

ISBN 978-0-521-72982-6 paperback

Editorial management: Gill Stacey

Cover illustration: 'Coalbrookdale by Night', 1801, by Philip Jacques de
Loutherbourg / Science Museum Pictorial.

Contents

Introduction   6

1 Approaching landscape and literature   11
Classical influences   11
Biblical influences: Eden and expulsion   15
The garden of love   18
The greenwood   20
Elegant shepherds   21
Symbolic nature   24
The 18th century: the Enlightenment   26
Towards the Romantics   31
Confinement and space   36
Assignments   39

2 Approaching the texts   40
Chaucer's landscapes   40
Shakespeare's landscapes   43
Marvell's ingenuity   46
Landscapes for elegy   49
Landscapes for religion   52
The country house   56
Romantic solitude   59
Landscapes of childhood   62
The Romantics: the sublime and the gothic   65
Hardy's Wessex   67
Observation and beyond   70
Working the land   73
Desolated land   76
Ancient and modern   79
Assignments   83

3 Texts and extracts   84
Simon Armitage
     from *Sir Gawain and the Green Knight*   84

Geoffrey Chaucer

    from *The Parlement of Foulys*   85

Thomas Carew

    'The Spring'   86

John Clare

    from *The Shepherd's Calendar*   86

Gerard Manley Hopkins

    'Spring'   87

John Milton

    from *Paradise Lost*   88

James Thomson

    from *The Seasons*   88

Dorothy Wordsworth

    from her *Journals*   89

Jane Austen

    from *Sense and Sensibility*   90

Percy Bysshe Shelley

    from 'Mont Blanc'   91

Matthew Arnold

    from 'The Scholar-Gipsy'   92

George Eliot

    from *The Mill on the Floss*   93

John Steinbeck

    from *The Grapes of Wrath*   94

D.H. Lawrence

    from *The Rainbow*   95

Edmund Blunden

    from *Undertones of War*   96

Stella Gibbons

    from *Cold Comfort Farm*   97

T.S. Eliot

    from *Four Quartets*   98

William Golding

    from *Free Fall*   99

Angela Carter

    from 'The Erl-King'   100

Ted Hughes
    from *Tales from Ovid*   101

4 Critical approaches   103
Political approaches   103
Feminist approaches   105
Ecological approaches   106
Assignments   109

5 How to write about landscape and literature   110
Responding to a poem   110
Responding to prose   111
Comparison   113
Preparing to write about a topic   115
Writing about the topic   117
Assignments   119

6 Resources   120
Further reading   120
Media resources: film and television   121
Websites   122
Glossary   122

Index   125
Acknowledgements   128

Introduction

One of literature's main delights is to provide readers with an escape from reality and into their imaginations. The poet John Keats saw this escape as a potentially fulfilling journey. In his sonnet 'On sitting down to read *King Lear* once again', he compares his re-reading of Shakespeare's play with travelling in a metaphorical landscape:

> When through the old oak forest I am gone,
> Let me not wander in a barren dream,
> But when I am consumed in the fire,
> Give me new Phoenix wings to fly at my desire.

The 'old oak forest' is a mysterious place with historical resonance. Keats is entering ancient Albion (an old word for England) where Lear was king. He expects the benefits of his journey to be spiritually passionate and life-changing.

Some other types of literary looking back are more peaceful, especially those that recall a pastoral Golden Age. It is often difficult to discover whether or not the authors really believed that such a time ever existed, but nostalgia for what is real or imagined is almost a necessary condition of being human. Each of us looks back to our own childhood, and each community recalls its collective past. What we see or remember may be part reality, part fiction. When recalling the past and appreciating its values, we may often feel uneasy about the progress that has been made since then; to our judgement it can seem not 'progress', but loss, regression or even a process of corruption.

Most writers whose journey takes them and their readers towards perfection describe it in terms of nature, as distinct from man-made civilisation. Much of the literature that celebrates a Golden Age, with all its simple innocence, has been written by educated men and women who live in courts or cities. Their myths of the past may be Christian, pagan or a subtle mixture of the two. It is often a paradox of their 'civilised' lives that they idealise their opposites: simple peasants in a pastoral landscape, where human nature is sustained by close affinity with the land – land which provides food to eat, scenic beauty to appreciate and leisure for love and meditation.

The status of landscape in art and literature

In the visual arts of the Renaissance, landscape held a low status. It was generally an accessory or background to the theme of the painting: for example, the crucifixion, John the Baptist preparing for his mission, Christ appearing to Mary Magdalene, St Jerome in the desert. The human situation, especially if religious, took centre stage and a central importance. Nor were artists concerned with accuracy when they painted the landscape. Many crucifixion scenes seem to take place not outside Jerusalem, but in the foothills of Tuscany or wherever the Italian or German artists lived. And even here they were not concerned to paint the authentic 'truth': rocks and trees, hills and valleys are rearranged to have a symbolic value (see Part 1, page 24) and, only then perhaps as a pleasing afterthought, simply to engage the eye.

The very word 'landscape' appeared late in the English language – in the early 17th century. A dictionary of 1612 describes *landtskip* as a Dutch word, in which the suffix *'-skip'* corresponds to the English *'-ship'*, as in 'friendship'. *Landtskip* was a term in painting where nature was included generally 'for the sake of something else'. However, the Dutch invented and developed the genre of landscape painting and the 1612 definition also suggests that a few artists were beginning to paint and draw the landscape for its own sake, for the pleasure of the view. Tastes have developed since 1612: there is no longer a hierarchy of subject matter in art to elevate heroic and religious subjects above nature.

Now that landscapes are more popular than any other subject, we may find it surprising that landscape was relegated in this way. After all, much early literature praised the secluded life. In the Bible, Christ went into the wilderness to focus his mind and prepare for his life's vocation. Ascetics, scholars and hermits, who very conspicuously place the mind above the body, have often withdrawn to the desert. Monasteries were built in remote places. And even today busy people go into the countryside on 'retreat' for spiritual nourishment. But in all these cases their aim is not *necessarily* to appreciate the landscape, which lies outside them, but rather to use the solitude they find in quiet settings to refresh the inner man or woman. It is therefore possible to find value in the countryside without really noticing what is there. Much pastoral poetry (see Part 1, page 21) refers generally to sheep, brooks, hills and sunshine as background to the poem's purpose, which is often a lover's longing.

Writing about time spent in remote places may have a double aim: first, to supply contrasts, philosophical or satirical, with public life; second, to educate the traveller who will then return to the main business of life in the court or city. They will have gained in wisdom not because they have contemplated the landscape, but because solitude there has allowed for self-contemplation.

John Milton was one of the first English poets to refer to 'landscape' or 'landskip'. He is celebrated chiefly for his serious and ambitious epic *Paradise Lost*, but in 1632, while still at Cambridge, he wrote the poem 'L'Allegro' (the cheerful man) as a lyrical light-hearted piece:

> Straight mine eye hath caught new pleasures
> Whilst the landskip round it measures;
> Russet lawns and fallows gray
> Where the nibbling flocks do stray;
> Mountains on whose barren breast
> The labouring clouds do often rest;
> Meadows trim with daisies pied,
> Shallow brooks, and rivers wide.

As with the 'catalogue' approach in much early pastoral poetry, there is no attempt here to dwell on any detail in the landscape or to pause for reflection. 'Lawns', 'flocks', 'mountains', 'clouds', 'meadows', 'brooks' and 'rivers' are all in the plural. Milton is restless: his attention bounds across the view, which seems typical of any natural scene rather than specific to one. But after all, he speaks with the voice of the lively, unthinking '*allegro*' man, for whom the beauty of the outdoors is a sort of generalised mood music. Milton is hardly suggesting that this frivolity can be the real business of life.

Land and landscape

When therefore does land become landscape? The answer is partly historical and partly a matter of taking a viewpoint. At first farmers took wild land and made it work for their purposes. They 'cultivated' it, a basic and specific part of our word 'culture', which has a much broader meaning. Later – but not until the late 18th century – tourists or cultured connoisseurs gave themselves a pleasing view of the land which their aesthetic sense then declared to be a picturesque landscape (see Part 1, page 29). Indeed, if they were artists, they could use the now-familiar pleasures of land arranged as landscape to create a painting.

Thus the land had been arranged twice: firstly in the visitor's chosen viewpoint; secondly in the artist's response to the view. The artist does not supply a direct imitation because the view is filtered and adapted by a discerning eye. We should call it a presentation rather than a representation, because paint as a medium both gives freedom and imposes constraints: artists are free to express their feelings but have to accept that their artefacts are not the same as the view in front of them. Thus artists are bound to modify and re-express what they see.

As with the visual arts, so with literature. Words are like paint: they can approximate to what the scene is like, but they can't reproduce it. Therefore good writers don't claim to deliver a likeness: they offer a version of the scene that may have a stimulus from real life, but it is better understood as being something newly created.

When the land becomes landscape it is, so to speak, consumed. Like the farmer who makes the land productive, the tourist and the artist are using and adjusting the land they see for their purposes. None is receiving or delivering nature as it is. All are controlling their environment by their toil, their eye or their skill.

This rearranging of nature may perhaps provide a setting for a myth, or idealise a lost world. It may demonstrate nature's power or delicacy, or create shock or wonder. It may give contextual meaning to the characters in the foreground of the story. It may help readers to step aside from the modern world, to slow down their lives, to observe detail and to connect with the sources of life.

How this book is organised

Part 1: Approaching landscape and literature

This part identifies the social, cultural and historical contexts of landscape in literature, from classical times up to 1900.

Part 2: Approaching the texts

Part 2 makes a thematic study of landscape in literature, from Geoffrey Chaucer to Simon Armitage.

Part 3: Texts and extracts

Part 3 contains texts and extracts from works discussed in this book or used as the focus for tasks and assignments. There is a distinct emphasis on works written after 1900.

Part 4: Critical approaches

This part considers some of the ways in which critics have written about landscape in literature.

Part 5: How to write about landscape and literature

Part 5 offers guidelines and assignments for those for whom this book is chiefly intended: students covering the topic as part of an advanced course in literary studies.

Part 6: Resources

This part contains guidance on further reading, media and web-based resources, a glossary and index. (Terms which appear in the glossary are highlighted in bold type when they first appear in the main text.)

At different points throughout the book, and at the end of Parts 1, 2, 4 and 5, there are tasks and assignments designed to help the reader reflect on ideas discussed in the text.

1 | Approaching landscape and literature

- How do classical and biblical texts influence landscape writing?

- What are the relationships between the visual arts and literature?

- What is the basis for idealised and symbolic landscape?

Classical influences

Idylls and eclogues

The *Idylls* of the Greek poet Theocritus (born *c.* 270 BC) are generally taken to be the source of the pastoral in western literature. An idyll originally meant a little shape or appearance and came to mean a short descriptive poem about the imagined life of herdsmen. 'Idyllic', meaning full of nature's charm, first appeared in the English language in the 19th century. The word also suggested a nostalgic ideal, allowing Theocritus to be adapted for contemporary needs. When Tennyson (1809–1892) wrote his *Idylls of the King* (about the legendary Arthur), he dedicated them to the recent memory of Prince Albert, who wore 'the white flower of a blameless life'.

Theocritus, using a version of rustic Greek dialect within the frame of more literary diction, was creating an elegant artifice for learned readers. His shepherds and goatherds invent **epigrams** and paradoxes, refer easily to gods and goddesses and sing serenades. Within the variety of his *Idylls* he included pastoral elegy (see Part 2, page 49): the most notable tells of a shepherd, Daphnis, who angered Aphrodite; he died young and nature shared in the general lament for his loss.

The Roman poet Virgil (70–19 BC) acknowledged Theocritus as a major influence when writing his *Eclogues*, but developed the pastoral form in his own ways: he refers to contemporary events, especially civil war, he identifies the shepherd with himself as poet, and gives more focus to nature's serenity than to the themes of human love. The terms 'eclogue' and 'idyll' often seem to be interchangeable, but eclogue often has the more specialised meaning of a dialogue in verse between shepherds or pastoral lovers. In his 1579 poem *The Shepherd's Calendar* (see page 22, below) Edmund Spenser made frequent use of dialogue form.

Though he plays with ideas of moral or political **allegory**, Virgil rarely commits himself in his *Eclogues* to much more than learned, playful elegance. However, later poets, wanting to absorb Virgil into their Christian culture, have paid special attention to the prophetic possibilities of *Eclogue 4*. He speaks of a child being born to coincide with a new Golden Age, 'All stains of our past wickedness being cleansed away'. Nature will rejoice and bring tributes:

> Child, your first birthday presents will come from nature's wild –
> Small presents: earth will shower you with romping ivy, fox-gloves,
> Bouquets of gipsy lilies and sweetly-smelling acanthus.
> Goats shall walk home, their udders taut with milk, and nobody
> Herding them: the ox will have no fear of the lion:
> Silk-soft blossom will grow from your very cradle to lap you.
> But snakes will die, and so will fair-seeming poisonous plants.

These lines can be taken to parallel stories of the Garden of Eden (see page 15, below) and Old Testament prophecies of Christ's birth. They also show nature seeming to behave in human ways, anticipating the widespread use of **pathetic fallacy** in much of the landscape writing that places human beings in the context of nature.

Virgil: the *Georgics*

Virgil lived through one of the most turbulent and defining periods of history. Julius Caesar was assassinated in 44 BC and the future of Rome hung in the balance until his adopted son Octavian defeated Mark Antony at the battle of Actium in 31 BC. Virgil saw Octavian (later named Augustus) as the saviour of Rome and his imperial rule as the guarantee of future peace and prosperity. He wrote the *Georgics* between 37 and 30 BC and dedicated the poem to the statesman Maecenas, who became a famous patron of the arts.

The *Georgics* was written to celebrate farming and its enduring values. Its four sections (on crops, trees, cattle and bees) were to be read also as practical and detailed handbooks on farming methods. What may seem to us as digressions – on Octavian's status and on political issues – were intended to place the whole work in the context of a fully flourishing community in which all parts of society contributed to peace and order. Indeed, the lower stratum (of farmers working close to the soil) supplied analogies for good political and moral discipline, designed to instruct Virgil's readers, the educated classes who could influence government.

The poem implied a warning for the decision-makers. Much of the land in Italy was threatened because the farms had been depopulated to provide soldiers for the wars. Later, veteran soldiers were rewarded with land from which many peasants had to be evicted. Both types of decision had disrupted the traditions of agriculture and also breached natural decorum by confusing the needs of the wars with the needs of the land. Virgil uses a military metaphor to show how good order has been lost: he describes how horses go wild, take charge of the chariot and 'force along the trembling charioteer'.

In one passage Virgil looks far into the future and imagines a ploughman on his land unearthing rusty weapons and 'mighty relics of gigantic bones'. It turns out that these are fragments from the great battle of Philippi when Octavian and Antony defeated Caesar's assassins, Brutus and Cassius. For Virgil's contemporaries this battle was a world-influencing event, but in the wider context of history its significance shrinks and it is the ploughman who will endure. Thomas Hardy imagined a similar perspective in his poem 'In Time of the Breaking of Nations', written in 1915, a year into the Great War. He wrote to express the paradox of how the humble outlasts the spectacular. The foreground shows 'Only a man harrowing clods', 'his old horse that stumbles and nods', the smoke from burning couch grass, and two lovers passing by; in the misty background Hardy hints at the half-forgotten stories of wars and European dynasties.

The *Georgics* became especially popular in 18th-century England, partly because of the political background: the memory of civil war; the execution of Charles I in 1649; the restoration of the monarchy by Charles II in 1660; the disputes about the succession in 1688; Marlborough's wars with France in the early 1700s. With national success came peace, the land could flourish and classical Roman values influenced all branches of the arts. This new Golden Age was known as 'Augustan', after Virgil's Emperor Caesar Augustus.

However, English readers of the *Georgics* knew what happened to Roman history after Virgil: the moral decline of Rome and the descent into barbarism. Values are precarious, not simply because life itself is bound to be transitory but because civilisation too may be fragile if men fail to be watchful. Poets have a particular duty to protect and assert these values, which are rooted in the practical life and discipline described in the *Georgics*. They should condemn great men when they fall short. Alexander Pope (1688–1744) was the greatest of the Augustan satirists; he attacked pretentious and lavish folly and celebrated the honest, simple life. In his 'Epistle to Lord Burlington' he exposes the empty splendour of 'Timon's' villa and predicts an ideal future:

> Another age shall see the golden ear
> Imbrown the slope, and nod on the parterre,
> Deep harvest bury all his pride has plann'd,
> And laughing Ceres reassume the land.

Pope anticipates here not Virgil's ploughman at the start of the year, but Ceres, the goddess of harvest, in a gold and brown autumn, delighted that she can 'reassume' authority over the land. Perhaps she is also mocking the pompous Timon, who currently owns it – but his tenure will be brief. Soon his grandiose house will be buried, like those relics of Philippi. Eventually the land will return to its more appropriate past, not as a natural wilderness before mankind appeared, but as an agricultural success. This means that people will still be in control, not – like Timon – for misguided display, but secure under the guiding principles of Ceres.

Ovid: the *Metamorphoses*

Ovid (43 BC–17 AD) lived in Rome under the Emperor Augustus until he was exiled for some unspecified offence; he then lived and died on the coast of the Black Sea. His *Metamorphoses* is a collection of stories gathered from Roman, Greek and Egyptian mythology – 'to tell of bodies which have been transformed into shapes of a different kind'. He describes the relationships of the gods with men and women, spanning from the time of the creation of the world out of Chaos, to his own times when the assassinated Julius Caesar was transformed into a heavenly star.

Ovid's Roman gods (notably Jupiter, Apollo, Diana, Mercury, Ceres) affect, and often afflict, human beings, by sharing our passions and frailties. Often they seem like erratic children, but with alarming power in their obsessions, lusts and resentments. It sometimes appears as though the gods too are subject to Destiny, just as humans are subject to the gods. It is not surprising that the focus of much Western literature, when authors are borrowing from the *Metamorphoses*, has been on the uncertainties inherent in life, love and death.

Out of the fifteen books of the *Metamorphoses* only the last four deal with the Trojan wars and later Roman history. Most of the work contains earlier **myths** and very few of these stories concern cities, wars or political life. They are overwhelmingly concerned with nature: myths of the sun, seas, harvest, vegetation, hunting. Primarily, Ovid wishes to convey the narrative force and the drama of his tale, but he also evokes a sense of the landscape, especially in the following:

- **Proserpina**, the daughter of Ceres, was dancing and gathering flowers with her nymphs, when Pluto, the god of the underworld, drove by in his chariot. No other goddess was prepared to abandon the sunlight and share his dark kingdom, so he abducted Proserpina. He carried her as far as the river Cyane, which began to seethe and roar to check his flight; thinking that Ceres would be pursuing, he struck a blow on the earth, which opened and let him pass through to his kingdom. Ceres searched fruitlessly for her daughter, and in rage damaged the fertility of the earth, until Arethusa, a nymph, spoke of seeing Proserpina as Pluto's queen. Jove, as arbiter, decreed that the husband had rights as well as the mother. He judged that Proserpina should spend six months in the underworld (winter) and six months with Ceres (summer).

- **Daphne**, the daughter of Peneus, a river god, attracted the love of Apollo. He tried to approach her gently but she fled from him until she reached a river. There, she begged her father to transform her and immediately she became a laurel tree. Apollo's love continued, but as a lasting honour to himself, celebrated poets and musicians were crowned with a laurel wreath. Special occasions in Rome – games, victory processions and religious festivals – were always sanctified with laurel.

- *Orpheus* was a wonderful musician who could tame even wild beasts and bring flowers into bloom. He fell in love with Eurydice, but at their wedding ceremony the torch held by Hymen, the god of marriage, smoked ominously. Soon afterwards a snake stung Eurydice's foot and her spirit descended to the underworld. Orpheus followed and his music charmed all who heard it, even Pluto, who restored Eurydice to him, provided that, on his journey back, he would not turn to look at her. He failed to obey this instruction and his wife vanished.

- *Actaeon*, a huntsman, came to a mountain spring to rest and drink the water. Diana (the goddess of the moon, of hunting and chastity) was there with her female attendants. She was bathing naked and was appalled to be seen by Actaeon. She threw water at his face; immediately antlers sprouted where the drops struck him, and he was transformed into a stag, only to be savaged to death by his dogs.

Ovid has always been widely read, especially by other poets who have alluded to his work and adapted it, most recently Ted Hughes in 1997 (see Part 3, page 101). The *Metamorphoses* was popular in the late Middle Ages and the (pagan) stories were often given Christian allegorical meaning: Apollo killing the python, for example, becomes Christ overcoming evil. Chaucer knew his work, as did Shakespeare, who used one of Ovid's tales for the episode of Pyramus and Thisbe within the play of *A Midsummer Night's Dream*, and the story of Medea's black magic for Prospero's renunciation of his powers in *The Tempest*.

Biblical influences: Eden and expulsion

The creation story (or myth) in the book of Genesis describes the first days of the world when God created the light, water, earth, plants, trees and animals. Finally, he created man 'after our likeness' (in his own image): 'Let him have dominion over the fish of the sea, and over the fowl of the air, and over the cattle, and over all the earth'. As the last of God's creative acts, man was the best. God then brought all the creatures before Adam, the very first man, who gave them their names. Naming is more than noticing or identifying: in some cultures, it may carry a type of verbal magic. In the Garden of Eden, it signified mastery and possession.

God placed Adam (and then Eve) in the Garden of Eden, both of them innocent amidst the profusion of nature.

> And the Lord God commanded the man, saying, Of every tree of the garden thou mayst freely eat:
> But of the tree of the knowledge of good and evil, thou shalt not eat of it: for in the day thou eatest thereof thou shalt surely die.

But Eve persuaded Adam to eat from the forbidden tree. In Genesis they pick 'fruit' from the tree; later traditions specified it as 'apple'.

In *Paradise Lost* (1667) Milton dramatises this moment:

> Earth trembl'd from her entrails, as again
> In pangs, and Nature gave a second groan,
> Sky lowr'd, and muttering Thunder, some sad drops
> Wept at completing of the mortal Sin
> Original …

The third 'character' in the story is the serpent that tempted Eve to eat the forbidden fruit first. It was 'more subtle than any other beast of the field which the Lord God had made'. In *Paradise Lost* Satan, wanting revenge on God, goes on a solitary mission to the newly created Earth. He enters the garden and then transforms himself into the serpent, so that he can prey on what Milton takes to be typical female frailties – her beauty, vanity, and her manoeuvres to gain power over a man.

Adam and Eve have become stereotypes in much Christian literature. Their story has been used to justify male authority and chauvinism, and most anti-feminist attitudes; and snakes generally provoke fear and disgust.

Adam's disobedience destroyed innocence and complicated the hierarchy of creation. **Renaissance** philosophers believed that from this act, known as The Fall, life became unpredictable; mankind now could sometimes aspire to the condition of angels and also fall to the level of beasts. Man and woman now had knowledge of evil, as well as good: behaviour and events would be confused; the earth would no longer yield its produce automatically; the climate would sometimes be harsh; suffering would be part of human destiny.

Even the assumption of human 'dominion' has become open to question. In modern times green movements sometimes use the Eden story to remind us that, since man was created last, nature came first and therefore has a primacy above men and a purity that should be respected. In specific terms, humans are polluting the earth and therefore continuing to disobey God or / and the principles of creation in newly disastrous ways.

The Song of Solomon

The Song of Solomon (or *Song of Songs*) from the Old Testament reads like an erotic poem of human love, generally as a dialogue between two lovers. It has also been interpreted allegorically as God's love for the Hebrew people, or Christ's love for the Church, or the perfected soul (personified as female) for the Word of God. The Alexandrian scholar Origen (185–254) believed that earthly love, which promises much, generally disappoints. But its archetype, which is God's love, always fulfils the soul's longing. And so the allegorical interpretation of *The Song* takes the reader through the earthly language and to the celestial meaning beyond.

The Song, or poem, is rich with imagery of plants, animals, fruits and spices. The land is made fertile by rivers, streams and fountains and offers up luxury for lovers to enjoy. Many of the ecstatic similes to describe the beloved are drawn from nature:

> this thy stature is like to a palm tree, and thy breasts are clusters of grapes …

> His cheeks are as a bed of spices, as sweet flowers: his lips like lilies, dropping sweet-smelling myrrh.

At the heart of the song is the *hortus conclusus* (the enclosed garden), which also supplies a strong precedent for medieval poets in their love stories. Their setting is always a version of **locus amoenus** and three archetypal gardens are likely to influence it:

- the Garden of Eden (see page 15, above)

- *Le Roman de la Rose* (see page 19, below)

- *The Song of Solomon*.

The Garden of Eden is biblical, *Le Roman de la Rose* is secular and literary, but the various interpretations of *The Song of Solomon* make it a hybrid work. This ambivalence parallels the uncertain language of much medieval love poetry. It seems to bridge pagan and Christian worlds. Many critics have commented on the 'religion' of love, how the lover seems almost to worship his lady, and how it is sometimes unclear whether he is addressing a courtly lady or the Virgin Mary.

The garden too is an ambivalent place, occupying somewhere between the wild and the cultivated. Nature ministers lavishly to men and women without anyone having to tend the land. However, there is always formality and control, especially when an archetypal garden is adapted for **fin amour**.

> A garden inclosed is my sister, my spouse; a spring shut up, a fountain sealed.
> Thy plants are an orchard of pomegranates, with pleasant fruits; camphire, with spikenard …
> … A fountain of gardens, a well of living waters, and streams from Lebanon.
>
> (Chapter 4, verses 12–15)

The garden of love

Late 14th-century England suffered the Hundred Years' War with France and several devastating outbreaks of plague – disasters that came near to ruining the economy. Yet there was also a great flowering of the arts under the royal patronage of Richard II (reigned 1377–1399) and aristocrats such as John of Gaunt. Money, time and energy were spent on the great English cathedrals, on music and display at court. Writers flourished too, as varied as Langland, Chaucer and the anonymous poet who wrote *Sir Gawain and the Green Knight*.

Dream poetry

Like many of their contemporaries, all three writers often told stories in their poems through dreams and visions. Some critics have argued that a dream is a way of escaping from grim reality; but the dream-poem is also a way of experimenting with visions of heaven or hell, of inventing a journey which educates the ignorant traveller, or (in more modern interpretation) of exploring the subconscious. Dream-literature has an origin in Christian mysticism; it also derives from French and Italian love poetry.

Typically, the poet recalls a dream, maybe a few years in the past, into which he plants a **persona** (the 'I' figure), who is often self-effacing and naive. This can be entertaining for the sophisticated poet and his courtly audience; but because the dreamer is also very receptive, it also provides a convenient ***tabula rasa*** for the experiences and landscapes of the dream. Sometimes the dreamer is led by an informative guide who can interpret what is seen; it is an important feature of most medieval writing that everything we perceive through our senses has a deeper spiritual meaning or counterpart, and, in particular, that the intense experiences of secular love may be related to the love of God.

One of Chaucer's most entertaining and thought-provoking dream-poems is *The Parlement of Foulys* (1382). The poet has been reading Cicero's *Dream of Scipio*, then, with imagination filled, he falls asleep and in his dream Scipio's guide appears to him. The dreamer (Chaucer's persona) is led to a gate on which the inscriptions point to the delights and despairs of love; he enters into a landscape so packed with plants and creatures that it feels more like a stylised tapestry than the real world (see Part 3, page 85). But this is not the world as we normally see it: this is a place as a dream might distort or intensify it, and as literary convention has handed it down to Chaucer.

The dreamer sees Cupid, Venus, Priapus, and personifications known to Chaucer's audience through *Le Roman de la Rose* – all of them unsettling or threatening – along with celebrated victims from history and mythology 'And al here love, and in what plyte they dyde'. He moves from the garden into a grassy place 'upon an hil of flouris', where the goddess Nature is about to preside over a debate amongst the birds about fidelity and *fin amour*. This is the point of the poem: the '*demande d'amour*' (the question about love). But this enclosed, and rather oppressive, space of the garden opens out into a wider space for the parliament, so that the opinions expressed have enough air to breathe and expand.

Le Roman de la Rose

Le Roman de la Rose, begun by Guillaume de Lorris (*c.* 1230) and finished by Jean de Meun (*c.* 1237), had an enormous influence on 14th-century European literature, second only to the Bible. It was translated into German and Italian – and part of it was also translated into Middle English, possibly by Chaucer.

It is an allegory of *fin amour*, telling of a young man who dreams that he walks on a May morning along the bank of the River of Life. He sees a walled garden, and eventually discovers the door to the garden, where the porter Idleness tells him that this is the garden of Delight, whose people relax and take pleasure in the shade of the trees. In the garden, he meets personifications of courtly life and then wanders away to enjoy the streams, animals and flowers. He is unaware that the god of Love is following him.

He reaches a fountain on which an inscription tells that this is where Narcissus saw his reflection and died for his love. The dreamer is alarmed but eventually looks into the water. At the bottom are two crystal stones that reflect a garden of roses nearby. Among the roses is a bud, not quite open. The dreamer reaches to pluck it, but the god of Love disables him with his arrows. The dreamer submits, does homage, becomes Love's servant – and thereby accepts the situation of being in love.

Service is painful and difficult; being in love is a craft involving great delicacy. The story describes setbacks and minor achievements for the dreamer, but always within the confines of the garden. Just as a medieval court is a complicated and artificial world in itself, so the garden of love in de Lorris' allegory may seem remote from real life. But the lover's psychology is detailed, and modern readers, when accustomed to the working of allegory, find the poem very sensitive to a lover's heightened sense of elation and despair.

For courtly poets and audiences (most poems were intended to be heard rather than read), *Le Roman de la Rose* was part of received knowledge. It could be used as a type of code. A springtime garden, gentle streams, heightened colours of flowers and grass, roses and lilies were all symbolic points of reference, not real conditions in any particular garden. When a poet mentioned them, they activated the whole genre of *fin amour* which de Lorris had started. The garden's formality was important too: it was an appropriate setting for the esoteric rules of court and the disciplines of service. In war a young man would serve his overlord; in peace he became a courtier showing obedience to his lady. Both types of service required discipline of a young man's powerful instincts: aggression to Mars, the god of war; sexual passion to Venus, the goddess of love.

The greenwood

The oak tree has always been associated with the robust, male English character, honest independence and individual liberty. England's pride was her navy and great ships were made of oak. It is no surprise that even today many village pubs are named after the oak – names such as The Royal Oak, Hearts of Oak.

Forests are more than national symbols. In Anglo-Saxon England there was little dense forest but there were many working woodlands with a vigorous local economy relating to towns, villages and settlements. Then the Norman Conquest brutally imposed forest law to reserve huge areas of woodland for the king's pleasure, to preserve game and to provide the sport of hunting for the aristocracy. The historian Simon Schama in his *Landscape and Memory* (1995) notes that 'the nomenclature "forest" that now replaced the older Latin terms of *saltus* or *silva* was in all probability derived from *foris*, or "outside"'.

The common people were largely dispossessed. A 16th-century summary of laws recorded the brutal penalty for killing a deer: 'the removal of both sets of soft organs: eyes and testicles'. Schama points out that in practice fines were more widespread and more useful – both to the crown, that always needed money for wars, and, in turn, to barons leasing the land. The barons allowed unscrupulous middlemen to fleece the commoners still further.

From these injustices there grew up the stories of Robin Hood, the outlaw who harassed corrupt officials but remained conservatively loyal to the king. His 'court' in the forest was based on decency, natural justice and honest English comradeship. Shakespeare's outlaws in *The Two Gentlemen of Verona* and *As You Like It* are based on these popular legends. The exiled Duke in *As You Like It* is said to 'live like the old Robin Hood of England … and fleet time carelessly as they did in the golden world'. Adam, well named as the honest old commoner who values tradition, is brought to the Duke who entertains him as an equal; the open-air feast in the forest is the ideal place for nature to validate the reciprocal values shared by the leader and his subjects.

Stories of Robin Hood first appeared in the repertoire of minstrels performing for aristocrats, and then became the subject of popular ballads. Robin and his men live in the greenwood and wear Lincoln green. Green is the colour of growth and renewal, as Robin, a sort of Lord of Misrule, uses law-breaking as a means of moral health to restore the land to the honest jurisdiction of the king. In 1515 Henry VIII, wanting to strengthen his contract with ordinary people, joined in the annual Robin Hood festivities.

Hunting

Robin and his men were not noblemen: they hunted deer to provide venison for their feasts. The aristocrats took possession of the forest also for hunting, but not with the focus on food. For them hunting was a manly blood-sport, an alternative to warfare and also, with its rules and hierarchy, a way of replicating the court out of doors. Young men would be initiated and accepted into the noble fellowship. In *As You Like It* Shakespeare includes an initiation scene in Act 4 and undercuts it with the satirical Jaques.

Genuine nobility obliges the young man to participate in the hunt – or 'the chase'. Theseus in Chaucer's *The Knight's Tale* and Sir Bertilak in *Sir Gawain and the Green Knight* are both great hunters. But if the young nobleman was unscrupulous his victims might be young women. In *Tess of the D'Urbervilles* (1891), Alec D'Urberville, an impostor whose family bought the ancient Norman title, takes Tess to The Chase – 'the oldest wood in England'. The fog descends and they lose their way:

> Darkness and silence ruled everywhere around. Above them rose the primeval yews and oaks of The Chase, in which were poised gentle roosting birds in their last nap; and about them stole the hopping rabbits and hares.

There Alec seduces her and destroys the rest of her life. The greenwood is innocent, though its greenness is temporarily covered by the dark mystery of the night; the human violation is made more gross by the gentleness of wildlife around them.

In George Eliot's *Adam Bede* (1859) Arthur Donnithorne, the young squire, meets Hetty Sorrel in woodland also known as The Chase, suggesting again that hunting is part of a noble English heritage. He begins his seduction there and completes it in the ironically named Hermitage, secluded among the fine old trees. Like Tess, Hetty has an illegitimate child. Being women, both are vulnerable and both are driven to their deaths following events in the very male territory of greenwood.

Elegant shepherds

In real life shepherds endure a hard practical existence, subject to unpredictable weather and to predators or diseases destroying their flocks. In Hardy's *Far from the Madding Crowd* (1874), subtitled a 'pastoral tragedy', Gabriel Oak is a shepherd who loses his flock and his livelihood, but who stoically endures all trouble and is granted a muted happiness in the final chapter.

But in Renaissance fiction the pastoral is rarely either tragedy or realism. It is a sunlit idyll of shepherds who seem to do no work, but who reflect on life and love in an idealised temperate landscape. The pastoral genre was borrowed from the classical eclogues of Theocritus and Virgil (see page 11, above), developed by the Italian poet Petrarch, then made popular in 16th-century England through two influential works: Edmund Spenser's *The Shepherd's Calendar* (1579) and Sir Philip Sidney's *Arcadia*.

Spenser gave the pastoral genre greater depth and variety, including a native English **vernacular** in some of the shepherds' speech. He also invented debates, as between an old shepherd who advocates discipline and a younger one who believes that life is made for pleasure and sexual adventure.

In *Love's Labours Lost* Shakespeare writes about young courtiers in love. He writes a typical pastoral poem, as from a shepherd, for one of these lovers to compose as a gift for his lady:

> On a day, (alack the day,)
> Love whose month was ever May:
> Spied a blossom passing fair,
> Playing in the wanton air.
> Through the velvet leaves the wind,
> All unseen gan passage find:
> That the shepherd (sick to death)
> Wished himself the heaven's breath.
> Air (quoth he) thy cheeks may blow,
> Air, would I might triumph so.
> But alas, my hand hath sworn,
> Ne'er to pluck thee from thy thorn.

Arcadia

The original inhabitants of Arcadia, a bleak area in the central Peloponnese, were reputed to be brutal and rapacious. Pan was their god, half-goat and half-man, encouraging promiscuity and disorder as well as uncontrolled fertility. His music, the pan-pipes, could lead to madness ('panic' is derived from his name). In their *Eclogues* Theocritus and Virgil softened Arcadia, and when the pastoral was revived in the Renaissance, the fictional place had totally departed from its origins: music, though now mellifluous and soothing, was all that remained.

Sidney's two versions of *Arcadia* (1581 and 1583) were prose romances dedicated to his sister, the Countess of Pembroke. They were combined into a hybrid form in 1593, seven years after his death. They contained songs and poetry in different verse forms, sometimes as dialogues between 'shepherds', some of whom are princes and nobility in rural retirement. Much of the writing is skilfully contrived, under the thin disguise of shepherds' lives, about lovers pleading for their lady's grace. The poet uses the setting not to locate the situation but to embroider a **conceit** about melancholy love, with as many careful correspondences as he can manage:

> My sheep are thoughts, which I both guide and serve:
> Their pasture is fair hills of fruitless love.
> On barren sweets they feed, and feeding sterve.
> I wail their lot but will not other prove;
> My sheephook is wanhope, which all upholds;
> My weeds desire, cut out in endless folds;
> What wool my sheep shall bear, whiles thus they live,
> In you it is, you must the judgement give.

Pastoral followers

A host of minor poets followed the fashion for pastoral in prose and drama as well as in poetry. Many were sophisticated craftsmen in language and they developed the pastoral as a stylish game, sometimes with complicated stories, often employing elegant conceits to express love and longing in a variety of moods. Anthologies were printed, some with elaborate titles: *The Paradyce of Daynty Devyses* (1576); *A Gorgeous Gallery of Gallant Inventions* (1578); *A Handefull of Pleasant Delites* (1584).

Perhaps the most famous is *England's Helicon* (1600), in which many of the poems were written to invite musical settings. Mount Helicon stood above the spring of water known as Hippocrene that inspired the muse of poetry; clearly Elizabethan England felt confident enough to compete with ancient Greece in artistic achievement. Pastoral verse, especially with Michael Drayton (1563–1631), was developing an English bias, referring to local games and customs and to more practical matters like the export of fleeces.

In some versions of the pastoral, the simplicity of the shepherd signified the purity of reason; compared with this, the court could seem devious, corrupt and self-serving. Thus pastoral could be used as allegory and satire to comment on social and political abuses. George Puttenham, a famous Elizabethan critic, wrote in his *Art of English Poesie* (1589): 'the Poet devised the Eclogue … not of purpose to counterfeit or represent the rustical manner of loves and communication: but under the veil of homely persons, and in rude speeches to insinuate and glance at greater matters'.

The anti-pastoral

Eventually idealism always seems to invite its realistic corrective. This is true of the pastoral, not in the sense of poets or artists offering 'real' landscapes, but of introducing stringent or dark elements into the idyll. Just as **pre-lapsarian** Eden had to end (see page 15, above) and a timeless existence was no longer possible for Adam and Eve, so the classical fiction of the shepherd's life was undermined by satire, old age or the intruding world of the city or court. Shakespeare's *As You Like It* (see Part 2, page 45) is one of the subtlest mixtures of the pastoral and anti-pastoral. The most famous pastoral poem, Christopher Marlowe's 'The Passionate Shepherd to his Love' (1588) became the basis for two anti-pastoral answers, one by John Donne, the other by Sir Walter Raleigh. Marlowe's shepherd promises perpetual delight to his girlfriend in a May-time landscape. Raleigh gives her sensible reply:

> If all the world and love were young,
> And truth in every shepherd's tongue,
> These pretty pleasures might me move
> To live with thee and be thy love
>
> But Time drives flocks from field to fold;
> When rivers rage and rocks grow cold;
> And Philomel becometh dumb;
> The rest complains of cares to come.

To seduce his girlfriend Marlowe had pretended that time could be halted. Raleigh's girl parodies the poem to show where time really leads us.

'*Et in Arcadia ego*': this is the title of two paintings by Guercino (1618) and Poussin (1639), later quoted by Evelyn Waugh in *Brideshead Revisited* (1945). Shepherds in a pastoral landscape come across a tomb with this inscription carved, as it were, by Death: 'Even in Arcadia I am present.' The idyll of permanent leisure for music, love and beauty must come to an end.

Symbolic nature

Words rarely have single and simple meanings: most carry baggage, some of it complicated. For example:

- they may be loaded with allusions gathered from previous usage

- even their broadly accepted meanings may shift imperceptibly over time

- they may carry cultural references that come and go with the collective memory.

A river may seem to be an uncomplicated idea, though it is easy to recognise that each one has its individuality: it may be fast, slow, deep, shallow, wooded, filled with boulders or vegetation. But a river is more than the way it looks. Moving water symbolises the passing of time and, in harmony with the changing seasons, it nourishes life. Therefore in *Hamlet,* when the Queen tells of Ophelia's suicide by the willow 'that grows aslant a brook' in a benign landscape, audiences reflect both on how changing times have changed her fortunes and on the irony of her choosing to die in a source of life.

Willows are associated with water and always have mournful associations. One of the most famous *Psalms* (137) begins:

> By the waters of Babylon, there we sat down, yea, we wept, when we remembered Zion.
> We hanged our harps upon the willows in the midst thereof.

This is a poem of exile, of bleak memory. In Shakespeare's *Othello* Desdemona, the rejected wife, about to die in a foreign land, sings a willow song passed down to her by her mother's maid, who also lost her lover. The willow came to be associated with chastity, typically about a maiden who died without lover or children.

Some types of symbolism have never been forgotten. The sun is associated with power, life and majesty; greenness with nature in general and with all types of ecology; the lion connotes power and the fox cunning; red roses indicate love; political leaders have been described as hawks or doves, depending on whether they urge aggressive or peaceful policies. Black has many associations, mostly negative (death, a black day, blackmail), though black political movements of the 20th century aimed to reinvent black as a positive.

Names have always carried resonance. Classical literature includes repeated stories of the pagan gods and goddesses to such an extent that their very names (even without the stories) operate as a type of shorthand to the reader who is in touch with that culture. The same is true for great names and events from history: Aeneas, Ulysses, Achilles – indeed any hero, Greek or Trojan, who fought in the Trojan War.

Since reading the classics and the Bible was fundamental to education in the western world up to 1900 and beyond, it was natural for writers to refer to these names and to assume that readers would understand. Our more fragmented culture in the last century has largely lost touch with our inherited classical background (and even in part with Christian stories and belief) and we need to make some efforts towards recovering our collective memory if we are to read with a rich understanding.

Here are some commonly used examples of symbolism in nature:

- **Dew** Since the dew falls mysteriously in the night, it takes on the silvery aspect of the moon. It appears in the morning and therefore symbolises youthful beauty, which old age will soon remove as the sun dries up the dew. It is often taken to be a sign of blessing, like the *manna* which appeared to Moses and his followers in the wilderness.

- **Lily** The lily is often a synonym for white: if applied to men it can connote cowardice but is more generally a female flower, associated with virginity, often with the brevity of life. Its chief Christian symbolism appears with the Annunciation, when the angel Gabriel appears to Mary. Pictorial art almost always shows a lily in his hand or in a vase beside Mary.

- **Poppy** The poppy is a narcotic, as when Keats writes of the 'poppied warmth of sleep' in 'The Eve of St Agnes'. A strong contemporary symbolism grew up after the First World War: we wear poppies on 11 November to commemorate the sacrifice of soldiers who died. The poppy looks like a splash of blood and (more literally) it grows in ground that has been disturbed, like the fields of Flanders. Isaac Rosenberg wrote of 'Poppies whose roots are in men's brains.'

- **Yew** The yew tree is generally found in graveyards. Ovid's path to the underworld is shaded by yews. More practically, the tree's strong, flexible branches made bows for the English archers who fought in the Hundred Years' War against France. In Shakespeare's *Richard II*, the king is aware of both dark uses for the tree when he refers to bows 'of double-fatal yew'.

Symbolism was especially popular in the Middle Ages and Renaissance, partly because it satisfies a human urge to make cross-references and to solve puzzles. More important, symbolic interpretation helps to bring coherence to the diversity in the world and to give moral direction to our responses.

This helps to explain the fashion for emblem books in the late 16th century. The first was Alciato's *Emblematum Liber* (1531). An emblem is a picture with a verbal explanation attached. One of Alciato's examples gave the motto *ex bello pax* above a beehive within a helmet; a set of verses completed the emblem to show how weapons of war may be turned into peace. The meaning of this optimistic emblem might remind readers of a similar prophecy in the book of Isaiah (2.4): 'and they shall beat their swords into ploughshares and their spears into pruning hooks'. This similarity helps to explain how, for example, the pre-Christian Virgil's hope for a new Golden Age (see page 11, above) could be merged with the coming of the Messiah, as foretold by the prophets. It is often through the serene and productive natural world that Christian and pagan writings come together.

The 18th century: the Enlightenment

English art and culture in the late 17th and 18th centuries became known as the **Enlightenment**. It was a guiding principle that Art should dominate and organise Nature, especially in the development of landscape gardening. Wealthy noblemen had their country estates transformed, according to guidelines borrowed from the moral authority of classical poets such as Virgil and Horace. Renaissance Italy also supplied precedents: the country villas that offered their owners therapeutic refreshment away from city life, and a refuge from the outbreaks of plague. Such villas were often in a hilltop setting that provided a view and a sense of commanding ownership.

'The genius of the place'

At the beginning of the 18th century, styles of landscaping were formal and symmetrical, following French practice and Palladian architecture. Then it became fashionable to introduce curves instead of straight lines and views were often unexpected instead of predictable. The poet Alexander Pope (1688–1744) explained this aesthetic principle:

> Let not each beauty everywhere be spied
> When half the skill is decently to hide.
> He gains all points who pleasingly confounds,
> Surprises, varies, and conceals the bounds.
>
> (from 'Moral Essay' to Lord Burlington)

This skilful manipulation ensured the fame of landscape gardeners such as William Kent (c.1685–1748), working for Lord Cobham at Stowe, and Lancelot 'Capability' Brown (1716–1783). These artists were moving taste towards the picturesque (see page 29, below).

To dominate nature was not necessarily to crush it. Pope spoke for the aesthetic vanguard when he urged artists to respond as well as to control. Just as a poet learns his craft through knowledge and imitation of the classics and then finds his own style, so an artist (having learned the principles) should merge his own individuality with nature's variety:

> Consult the genius of the place in all
> That tells the waters or to rise or fall
> Or helps th'ambitious hill the heavens to scale
> Or scoops in circling theatres the vale ...
> Calls in the country, catches opening glades,
> Joins willing woods, and varies shades from shades.
>
> (from 'Moral Essay' to Lord Burlington)

'Genius' is used here in its original meaning of 'guardian spirit'. Just as a person is born with an individual soul, so a place has its spirit or deity, a belief common in pagan cultures as well as in the 'enlightened' 18th century. What Pope advises here can be achieved only by sensitive intuition; mere rules of art would be too crude to capture the spirit and to work with it.

The arts are interconnected: a poet could become an expert in landscaping; it was also perfectly appropriate for Joseph Addison to compare reading books to travelling in nature:

Reading the *Iliad* is like travelling through a country uninhabited, where the fancy is entertained with a thousand savage prospects of vast deserts, wide uncultivated marshes, huge forests, misshapen rocks and precipices. On the contrary the *Aeneid* is like a well-ordered garden … but when we are in the *Metamorphoses*, we are on enchanted ground, and see nothing but scenes of magic lying around us.

(from 'Essay on the Pleasures of the Imagination', *Spectator* 1712)

These lines observe an 18th-century belief in balance: the books which dominate everyone's education are the great classical works, but these can be read and applied in new ways. As Pope advised, the poet's job is to convey 'What oft was thought but ne'er so well expressed.' He must cherish the old and also respond to the needs of his own times.

Claude Lorrain

The artist Claude Lorrain (1600–1682) was born as Claude Gelée in the French province of Lorraine and studied in Rome and Naples. He placed classical subjects, like scenes from Virgil's *Aeneid*, in elegantly arranged natural settings. These were so evocative that the landscape became valued for its own sake and not simply as an adjunct to 'higher' subjects like history and great literature. Working in the Campagna near Rome encouraged him into a sense of the past; his landscapes are nostalgic, though also carefully observed with naturalistic detail. Claude believed in carefully defined planes of vision, encouraging the eye to travel through a dark foreground to settle on the distant horizon, often with a silvery light that seems to transfigure the scene.

It was a typical 18th-century practice for wealthy young English noblemen to travel in Italy on what was known as The Grand Tour. This helped to create a fashion for Claude's work in England (along with that of Poussin and Salvator Rosa), even to the extent of having their grounds at home landscaped in the style of his painting. Many engravings were made of his works; his style and methods did much to influence aesthetic theory.

18th-century tourists and amateur artists in the (later) picturesque style often travelled with a Claude Glass (also known as a Black Mirror). It had a four-inch convex shape that confined the view and diminished colour, so giving extra value to its tonal gradations. They would turn away from a scene and appreciate it through the glass, which gave it soft tints as in a picture by Claude. Its use was advocated by William Gilpin (see page 29, below). Whereas Claude had taken his artistic inspiration from nature, now connoisseurs judged nature according to how well it arranged itself to the standards of his art. This paradox was mocked by satirists of what seemed to them a new aesthetic affectation; they found it amusingly absurd that tourists, having found an especially fine view, should turn their backs on it.

John Ruskin, the great 19th-century art critic, opposed Claude and his followers for idealising and therefore misrepresenting nature. His *Modern Painters* (1843–1860) is a passionate appeal for truth in observation, and he seized on one of Claude's landscapes, set at evening in the Roman Campagna, to write his own more honest version of the painting:

> Let the reader imagine himself for a moment withdrawn from the sounds and motion of the living world, and sent forth alone into this wild and wasted plain. The earth yields and crumbles beneath his foot, tread he never so lightly, for its substance is white, hollow and carious, like the dusty wreck of the bones of men (*a footnote adds at this point*: The vegetable soil of the Campagna is chiefly formed by decomposed lavas, and under it lies a bed of white pumice, exactly resembling remnants of bones). The long knotted grass waves and tosses feebly in the evening wind, and the shadows of its motion shake feverishly along the banks of ruin that lift themselves to the sunlight. Hillocks of mouldering earth heave around him, as if the dead beneath were struggling in their sleep; scattered blocks of black stone, four-square, remnants of mighty edifices, not one left upon another, lie upon them to keep them down. A dull purple poisonous haze stretches level along the desert, veiling its spectral wrecks of massy ruins, on whose rents the red light rests, like a dying fire on defiled altars.
>
> (quoted by Malcolm Andrews in *Landscape and Western Art*)

▶ Some critics argue that Ruskin's 'accurate' version of the landscape becomes as much an invention as Claude's painting. Do you agree with this view?

Gilpin and the picturesque

William Gilpin (1724–1804) was a schoolmaster, clergyman and author of works on English landscape, which he illustrated with his own aquatint engravings. He is generally recognised as founding the cult of the picturesque, which he defined as 'that kind of beauty which is agreeable in a picture'.

He grew up in Cumbria, where his father was an amateur artist, which perhaps encouraged his special love of mountain scenery, especially when it is rugged, intricate and varied. In 1794 he wrote:

> … the wild and rough parts of nature produce the strongest effects on the imagination; and we may add, they are the only objects in landscape which please the picturesque eye. Everything trim, and smooth, and neat, affects it coolly.

His new category of picturesque, somewhere between the beautiful (which is smooth and relaxing) and the sublime (which disturbs), depended on several guidelines, which some of his followers turned into rules. He had opinions on composition, light and shade, distance and foreground, darker screens, as often provided by trees at the sides of the picture. He deplored anything vulgar, like cottages, and also avoided the firm, clear lines of modern buildings. He approved of ruins in a picturesque view, not just for their dignity, but because their broken lines seemed to naturalise them into the land – even though they were originally man-made:

> ... a pile in a state of ruin receives the richest decorations from the various colours which it acquires from time. It receives the stains of weather; the incrustations of moss; and the varied tints of flowering weeds.

In this observation Gilpin's aesthetic sense was close to the gothic (see page 34, below).

Gilpin was developing his theories at a time when domestic tourism was increasing. From the early 1780s, moves towards revolution in France were limiting opportunities for foreign touring. Improved roads in England made it easier for families to travel. The well-to-do visited not only fashionable towns like Bath, but also areas of rural beauty – Cumbria, the Scottish Highlands, North Wales, the Wye Valley. Good taste could apply to the country as it could to towns, and those who wished to be thought cultured turned Gilpin's picturesque principles into a fashion. For women, in particular, drawing and appreciation of landscape became a necessary accomplishment, along with music, dancing, embroidery and reading.

Criticising the picturesque

Fashion is always open to satire and so Gilpin became a target, especially in a series of cartoons about an elderly Dr Syntax, a shambolic clergyman who careered across the countryside on horseback looking for picturesque views, completely oblivious to common sense and to life around him. Jane Austen also makes some sharp remarks about the picturesque cult, but in *Pride and Prejudice* (1813) her sensible heroine Elizabeth Bennett is preparing to visit the Lake District with her aunt and uncle. She, at least, can distinguish between true feeling and fashionable affectation. They get as far as north Derbyshire, which also has enough fine landscape to please both her and William Gilpin.

It is perhaps fairer to mock the pretensions of his more shallow followers than Gilpin himself. He was clear that nature 'works on a vast scale; and, no doubt, harmoniously, if her schemes could be comprehended'. The artist, who lives and thinks on a merely human scale, accepts limitations and 'lays down his little rules'. But for Gilpin both nature and art are concerned with coherence and harmony. In this respect he was typical of his 'enlightened' age. Though his preferred mountain landscapes were wild enough to approach the 'sublime' (a word he often used), he was still an 18th-century man of taste, detached and objective in his judgements. He valued the imagination, but confined its operation to particular scenes. Wordsworth's romanticism in the 1790s made much greater claims for the imagination – as a moral and spiritual force that penetrated beyond what the eye can see.

Critics of the picturesque point out that its exclusively aesthetic principles evade the conditions of real life and nature: accurate observation; dwelling in a particular place; economic realities; people who have to make a living from the land.

The tourists' need to make pictures both evades the truth and asserts control. They turn the land into a commodity, requiring nature to fit in with human tastes. It is ironic that Wordsworth, whose deep empathy with nature was as great as any other poet's, sold more copies of his *Guide to the Lakes* than his volumes of verse. Though valuing solitude, he did more than anyone to promote tourism in the Lake District.

Nature as picturesque continues today in our constant use of rectangular frames: the art gallery, the television, cinema and computer screen, the camera's viewfinder. All are types of window behind which we can enjoy a sense of control, gadgetry and civilised comfort to ensure that our chosen ways of seeing create (rather than simply respond to) the world around us.

Towards the Romantics

Rousseau

Jean Jacques Rousseau (1712–1778), who was born and died in Switzerland, wrote on politics, philosophy and education, challenging the values of civilisation which he found in France during the so-called Enlightenment (see page 26, above). His *Social Contract* (1762) was admired and constantly quoted by supporters of the French Revolution (1789–1792) and *Emile,* a novel written in 1760, influenced liberal experiments in education.

His contemporaries believed that the innate powers of reason distinguished men from animals and produced all the advances of human civilisation. But Rousseau maintained that 'man is born free' of the 'chains' that have confined him through the course of human history. He believed that freedom is fundamental for all human life and that reason has been merely an acquired faculty, leading to misery as much as to material progress.

In 1754 he wrote *Discourse on the Origin and Foundations of Inequality among Men*, which asserts that man was closest to his real nature when primitive and on the level of other animals.

> I see him satisfying his hunger under an oak tree, quenching his thirst at the first stream, finding his bed at the foot of the first tree that supplied his meal; and thus all his needs are satisfied.

He traces mankind's development from the first 'indolent' stage to a more active state, which followers of Rousseau have described as the 'noble savage':

> ... this state is the veritable youth of the world; ... all the subsequent progress has been in appearance so many steps toward the perfection of the individual, and in fact toward the decay of the species.

He believes that decay began not with gold and silver, but at an earlier stage: with iron and wheat. Both developments led to property, individual ambition, aggression and therefore to inequality. Whereas Virgil praised the self-denying life spent in cultivating the land, Rousseau is far more severe and anticipates the deep ecology (see Part 4, page 106) of those Greens who idealise the American wilderness and those who live outside urban values, such as the native American Indians or the aboriginal peoples of Australia.

Rousseau's investigation into origins anticipated in some ways Darwin's theories in *The Origin of Species* (1859) and also contributed much to the attitudes of the **Romantics**, especially to their libertarian political views. Wordsworth and Coleridge, for example, were politically active in the 1790s: they supported the principles of the French Revolution and they envisaged a society of true communal values in which property and exploitation would have no place.

Rousseau did not idealise primitive mankind as living in some idyllic Golden Age. He acknowledged that life was often harsh and painful, rather like the training given to young men in Sparta to make them tough and resilient. Like animals, human beings follow their powerful instincts, but, unlike animals, they have free will. This freedom can be abused. People have used it to acquire material wealth and self-indulgent comforts, which the Spartans deplored. Rousseau warned against the abuses of freedom, which have led to diseases, decadence, tyranny and threats to the green health of the land.

Rousseau's radical thinking, particularly towards the land, coincides with that of several Romantic poets:

- Wordsworth's concern for the dispossessed who have returned to communion with the land: as in 'The Pedlar' and 'The Cumberland Beggar'.

- *Lyrical Ballads (1798)* in which Wordsworth and Coleridge value the instincts and insights of childhood. Children becoming adults are like men who live close to nature, then move into cities.

- John Clare, distressed by the enclosure of common land, feels estranged from his childhood. He describes his loss in 'The Flitting', and writes with great empathy in *The Rural Muse* about vulnerable birds and animals dwelling in their natural environment.

All these poets, like many Romantic artists, separated themselves from society, either because they were solitary by nature or because they were hostile to society's customs and beliefs. This was also the case with Rousseau in his last years. His final work, *Reveries of the Solitary Walker* (1782), speaks of retreating into his own memory and imagination, stimulated by a communion with unpeopled nature.

Burke and the sublime

Edmund Burke (1729–1797) was a lawyer and Whig statesman. He was known internationally for his *Reflections on the French Revolution* (1790), but had already made an impact on literary criticism through his *Philosophical Enquiry into the Origin of our ideas on the Sublime and Beautiful* (1757).

Burke cannot be classed as a Romantic thinker, but his views on the sublime anticipated theorists such as Gilpin (see page 29, above), the principles of gothic (see page 34, below) and the creative imagination of Wordsworth, Coleridge and Shelley. The concept of the sublime was already well known, chiefly through the Greek philosopher Longinus and the 17th-century French critic Boileau.

Burke's contribution was to argue that a frisson of pain and danger are necessary sources of the sublime. Whereas beauty implies pleasure, smoothness and a human scale, the sublime contains terror, ruggedness and magnitude. Sublime landscape may be found in a vast wilderness, generally with mountains; one reacts with astonishment rather than simple pleasure. The English Lake District and, even more, the Swiss Alps, would become sources of the sublime for later 18th-century tourists. Sublimity, unlike the picturesque, depends on disorientation: the reader or spectator is taken close to disaster but also knows he is safe; he is both disturbed and reassured. Readers and travellers often use oxymorons, such as 'a delightful horror, a terrible joy'. Experiencing the sublime is the opposite of Enlightenment clarity and control.

The sublime does not exist merely in scenery or events. It depends on the individual's subjective imagination, a creative force that is stimulated by sensory experiences. Wordsworth was to take this theory further in his belief that Nature works as a creative principle through the world around us to expand the soul.

> And I have felt
> A presence that disturbs me with the joy

Of elevated thoughts; a sense sublime
Of something far more deeply interfused,
Whose dwelling is the light of setting suns,
And the round ocean and the living air,
And the blue sky, and in the mind of man:
           (from 'Lines composed a few miles above Tintern Abbey', 1798)

These lines do not convey the details of landscape; their visual effects are generalised and the verse is strongly aural. Burke believed that poetry and **rhetoric**, more than painting, are likely to convey the sublime because 'their business is to affect rather by sympathy than imitation'. Painting, being more precise, is therefore less suggestive; the responding imagination is stimulated more by language than by visual effects. Burke lists 'God', 'angels', 'devils', 'heaven' and 'hell' to suggest that these vast and alarming ideas have an effect on the passions rather than the intellect. He finds sublimity in Milton and quotes from *Paradise Lost*:

Through many a dark and drearie Vale
They passed, and many a Region dolorous,
O'er many a Frozen, many a Fierie Alpe,
Rocks, Caves, Lakes, Fens, Bogs, Dens, and shades of death
A Universe of Death …

Burke believes that the imprecision in the phrase 'a Universe of Death' gives sublimely terrifying force to the journey described in the preceding lines.

Burke was widely read. The value he placed on imprecision appealed to Coleridge who disparaged 'dutchified' poetry with its minute touches of realistic detail and felt that 'the power of poetry is by a single word, perhaps, to instil energy into the mind'. Wordsworth acknowledged Burke, but not slavishly. However, Blake dismissed Burke's ideas, thinking them too rooted in the sensations and not enough in visionary inspiration.

Gothic

The Goths were a group of tribes that ravaged Europe around the end of the Roman Empire and contributed to what became known as the Dark Ages. As an artistic term, 'gothic' is most prominent in describing styles of European architecture, especially that of monasteries, churches and cathedrals from the 12th to the 16th centuries: vast, high buildings, often very dark but with striking effects of light through arched windows. After the Reformation they became associated with Catholic 'superstition', as distinct from the more open Protestant preaching churches.

In the 17th and 18th centuries, often described as the Enlightenment or Age of Reason, gothic became synonymous with crude barbarism and lack of taste, even though the true medieval gothic was highly sophisticated. But to disparage something often gives it a forbidden glamour and therefore elements of the gothic persisted through these more rational times.

Darkness, death and sensational events have often fascinated readers and audiences, as with the Jacobean genre of revenge tragedy. Antonio, in John Webster's *The Duchess of Malfi* (1614), a play dominated by psychologically damaged characters, enjoys the melancholy of such places, where he is to hear his murdered wife speak to him as an echo from the walls:

> I do love these ancient ruins.
> We never tread upon them but we set
> Our foot upon some reverend history ...
>   All things have their end:
> Churches and cities, which have diseases like to men,
> Must have like death that we have.

The 18th century developed the gothic substantially as an undercurrent of pre-romantic feeling that valued much that was irrational: a taste for fantasy, sensationalism, superstition and horror. Interest in the Middle Ages became a cult, especially as ruins of great medieval buildings could be seen, often in remote, wooded landscapes. In 1717 Alexander Pope, the Augustan poet, wrote a verse letter from 'Eloisa to Abelard', recalling one of the great tragic love stories of the Middle Ages.

1764 was a significant year in the English gothic revival. Horace Walpole published *The Castle of Otranto*, a tale of extreme passion and horror, including ghosts, a dark vault, an eerie forest cave, a tyrant, a mysterious knight, a living statue and innocent maidens. William Beckford (1759–1844) inherited a vast fortune, which he used to build a huge gothic castle at Fonthill near Salisbury Plain; he also wrote his own horror story, *Vathek* (1782). He claimed that the story was 'so horrid that I tremble whilst relating it and have not a nerve in my frame but vibrates like an aspen'.

A wave of gothic fiction followed, notably Ann Radcliffe's *The Mysteries of Udolpho* (1794) and Matthew Lewis' *The Monk* (1796). The novel which survives most enduringly today is Mary Shelley's *Frankenstein* (1818). Gothic themes and conventions also appear in many other works: Coleridge's *The Ancient Mariner* (1797–1798) and 'Christabel' (1798–1799), novels by the Brontë sisters, stories by Edgar Allen Poe, some of Charles Dickens' settings in prisons and gloomy houses, Wilkie Collins' *The Woman in White* (1860), Bram Stoker's vampire story *Dracula* (1890).

There are gothic elements in 20th-century authors, such as Iris Murdoch and Angela Carter. Wherever there are settings in dark forests, graveyards, remote castles, ruins of holy places as background for strange stories or to encourage morbid meditation beyond the realms of reason, there is likely to be some trace of the gothic.

Confinement and space

Enclosure

From around 1750 landowners' private petitions led to Acts of Parliament that permitted them to enclose common land so that agriculture could be more efficient. So many of these acts went through complicated and expensive procedures that in 1836 and 1840 General Enclosure Acts were passed to enable landowners to enclose land without reference to parliament.

There were two types of enclosure:

- common grazing land was taken over either to improve the stock of animals or to be turned into arable land

- arable land was divided up into larger fields and reallocated to landowners.

There grew up a new professional class of tenant farmer who had to make the land more productive to pay the high rents – rents that would in turn compensate the landowner for his time and legal expenses.

Before enclosure most parishes consisted of a circular area of land with its village at the hub; few people travelled and the parish was a very stable and cohesive unit with its local customs. After enclosure, the newly professional farming business needed good roads to connect the larger market towns. Gradually the parishes and their villages lost some of their local significance and became merely staging points within a much larger agricultural economy.

Some economic historians argue that enclosure provided the wealth that increased wages and employment opportunities for the poor. In some areas the land acquired more interesting features that made it picturesque for tourists, especially when productive farming took its place amidst woods and hills (see the extract from *Sense and Sensibility*, Part 3, page 90).

Easier travel helped to extend people's mental, as well as physical horizons, but there was also a heavy emotional price to pay for these 'improvements'. If a parish lost its traditional sense of identity, its people lost their sense of dwelling – in other words, the uniqueness of place where man and local nature are as one.

The poet John Clare (see Part 2, page 72) was uprooted from his parish of Helpston in Northamptonshire and moved a very few miles to Northborough. His sense of alienation is evident in these lines:

> And Crossberry Way and old Round Oak's narrow lane
> With its hollow trees like pulpits, I shall never see again;
> Inclosure like a Bonaparte let not a thing remain,
> It levelled every bush and tree and levelled every hill
> And hung the moles for traitors – though the brook is running still,
> It runs a naked brook, cold and chill.

Note how the place names give intimate identity to his memory and how 'levelled' suggests that the land now becomes impersonal. In the early 19th century Napoleon (Bonaparte) had the reputation of a bogeyman in England. Clare could hardly have found a more extreme simile than to compare his devastation of Europe with landowners destroying traditional England. Clare's poem 'The Flitting' (1832) gives the fullest account of his feelings about enclosure; he gave it the subtitle 'On Leaving the Cottage of my Birth'.

19th-century contexts

Anthony Trollope entitled one his novels *The Way We Live Now* (1875), an apt description of what many 19th-century authors held as a principal aim: to describe the state of England and, often through satire and irony, to comment on abuse and inequality. Many novels are set in a particular region, where the landscape contributes to the characters' social and moral contexts. In *Middlemarch* (1871) George Eliot is both literal and symbolic: the title indicates that the action is set in the midlands (her home area of Warwickshire) and that her broad range of characters and action represent the centre of national concern.

Several 19th-century novelists are associated with particular regions, though their work often ranges more widely:

- Emily and Charlotte Brontë with the bleak landscape of Yorkshire and north Derbyshire

- Elizabeth Gaskell with the industrial north, making sharp contrast in *North and South* (1855) with the softer landscapes and lifestyles of Hampshire

- Thomas Hardy with south-western counties of England, which he calls 'Wessex' (see Part 2, page 67)

- Anthony Trollope, in his Barsetshire novels, with semi-rural privilege in a fictitious southern cathedral town

- Jane Austen with Hampshire and prosperous small towns such as Bath and Lyme Regis.

Most of these writers use conventional storytelling methods, either through an omniscient narrator or a first-person narrative. They delineate a range of realistic characters and place them in settings that have clear social implications and are easy to visualise. For example, in the opening chapters of *Great Expectations* (1860–1861) Dickens describes the windswept Kent marshes, which are made more terrifying by the horror-story technique of having a small boy tell of being threatened by an escaped convict:

The marshes were just a long black horizontal line then, as I stopped to look after him; and the river was just another horizontal line, not nearly so broad nor yet so black; and the sky was just a row of long angry red lines and dense black lines intermixed …

Dickens shows aesthetic judgement in the surprising technique of having the boy 'paint' the scene as an artist might; the scene also becomes retrospectively useful as he develops his views of the justice system and how criminals are treated.

Thoreau: *Walden*

The American writer Henry David Thoreau (1817–1862) wrote *Walden* (1845–1847) to describe his experiment in self-sufficient living beside Walden pond near Concord in Massachussetts. The book received only slight public regard in its day, but it soon came to be recognised as a literary masterpiece for Thoreau's evocative insights into nature and his radical philosophy, questioning American materialism and work ethic. It influenced worldwide attitudes to the wilderness, the growth of modern ecology movements and the system of American national parks. It also helped to foster the American frontier spirit of rugged manhood and has become an important text in American education in helping to define the nation's character. Its independent spirit, resisting conformity, influenced even Ghandi and Martin Luther King.

Thoreau's philosophy often coincides with Wordsworth's, as in his attitude to the responsiveness of children: 'I have always been regretting I was not as wise as the day I was born.' He takes a radical and primitive approach to time, not filling it anxiously with busy-ness, but instead he feels fulfilled in tending his field of beans or in sitting at his door watching and hearing nature around him. He values each day's dawn both for its silent beauty and also for the moral reawakening it encourages. He watches the lake and feels engaged by it, much as Rousseau did beside Lake Geneva: 'A lake is the landscape's most beautiful and expressive feature. It is the earth's eye; looking into which the beholder measures the depth of his own nature.'

The book is satirical as well as evocative. In his opening section entitled 'Economy', Thoreau attacks many assumptions of contemporary life:

It is the luxurious and dissipated who set the fashions which the herd so diligently follow.

It would be some advantage to live a primitive and frontier life, though in the midst of an outward civilisation, if only to learn what are the gross necessaries of life and what methods have been taken to obtain them.

… we know not what it is to live in the open air, and our lives are domestic in more senses than we think. From the hearth to the field is a great distance. It would be well perhaps if we were to spend more of our days and nights without any obstruction between us and the celestial bodies, if the poet did not speak so much from under a roof, or the saint dwell there so long. Birds do not sing in caves, nor do doves cherish their innocence in dovecots.

By avarice and selfishness, and a grovelling habit, from which none of us is free, of regarding the soil as property, … the landscape is deformed, husbandry is degraded with us, and the farmer leads the meanest of lives. He knows Nature but as a robber.

Assignments

1   Compare the Genesis story of creation (see page 15, above) with Ovid's account in *Metamorphoses* and with creation myths from any other cultures and religions.

2   Compare the methods and language of Rousseau, Wordsworth, Clare and Thoreau in the values they find in primitive and naive living.

3   Read the extract from Shelley's *Mont Blanc* (Part 3, page 91). How far does this exemplify Burke's views on the sublime (see page 33, above)?

4   Argue for and against the opinion that being 'true to nature' is an irrelevant criterion when an artist uses his creative imagination.

2 | **Approaching the texts**

- How do major authors use landscape to support their themes and characters?

- How does landscape reflect social conditions and conventions?

- How far is accurate observation important in depicting landscape?

Chaucer's landscapes

Geoffrey Chaucer (*c.*1342–1400) was a court poet and, though he could write in different styles about a wide social range within contemporary society, most of his stories reflect the concerns of noble life. He inherited and used the tradition of medieval romance in which each narrative is set not in a particularised place but in a conventional setting (or *topos*), such as a garden, castle, court, forest, by a river or in a meadow.

The Knight's Tale

Each *topos* carries an implied meaning that is more significant than a precisely observed place could provide. In *The Knight's Tale*, the *topos* – the grove outside Athens – is seen first in a typical May-time setting appropriate for ardent love; then it becomes a battleground for Arcite and Palamon, the two young knights, both in love with Emily. When Duke Theseus reaches the place he sees them fighting like two forest boars. Their rivalry has seemed to reduce them to wild animals. But their motive is love, which is potentially an ennobling influence, and so Theseus decrees that their conflict must be repeated as a great tournament in a year's time. He will build a magnificent stadium that will include temples to Mars, Venus and Diana (who receive worship from Arcite, Palamon and Emily).

Most of the landscape in *The Knight's Tale* is found in murals in these temples. This removes it even further from reality than the May-morning *topos*. Chaucer's literary art describes a painter's art, which has turned unsettling landscapes into symbolic attributes of stern and powerful gods. Mars, the god of war, is given the most frightening scene of all:

> First on the wal was peynted a forest,
> In which ther dwelleth neither man ne best,
> With knotty, knarry bareyne trees olde
> Of stubbes sharpe and hidouse to biholde;
> In which ther ran a rumbel and a swough,
> As though a storm sholde brosten every bough

These murals use landscape to help explain a powerful purpose in this tale. We all live in a world of suffering and loss governed by chance and by gods who have alarming power but no more wisdom than we have. If we are to assert ourselves, rather than endure bleak lives and die like animals, we must construct an ordered society. And so Duke Theseus issues decrees, erects great buildings, commissions art and uses publicity, all acting as bulwarks against pain and disaster. He doesn't ignore what is negative but faces it, as shown in the temples' landscape murals, and acknowledges its presence within his positive vision of how life should be lived.

Theseus' vision especially celebrates social and personal qualities such as *fin amour* and *gentilesse*. A *gentil* knight or young squire is steadfast in war and generous in peace. He behaves with grace and sensitivity to others and when he loves a lady his *gentil* qualities are raised to a new level of devoted service. Essentially, *gentilesse* is an aristocratic virtue, and in *The Franklin's Tale* Chaucer explores and tests it through various critical moments in the narrative.

The Franklin's Tale

The lady Dorigen, recently married to a knight, Arveragus, becomes anxious for his safety on a voyage to England. She is fixated on some black rocks which may threaten his ship. The rocks are real and they also symbolise her 'derke fantasye'. She is persuaded to join other ladies in a beautiful garden, where they 'pleye hem al the longe day.' Essentially, the garden is a female place, as in *Le Roman de la Rose*, but young men also participate there in dances, games and all the elegant pastimes of courteous life, where leisure has been turned into an art form. Among them is Aurelius, as obsessively in love with Dorigen as she is cast down by the black rocks. Their intensity of feelings and misguided judgement leads to a very unwise bargain: she will become his lover if he will remove the black rocks from the sea.

Chaucer's description of the garden is generalised, but its meanings – through a type of literary shorthand – would be evident to his audience who understood the conventions of romance:

> And this was on the sixte morwe of May,
> Which May hadde peynted with his softe shoures
> This gardyn ful of leves and floures;
> And craft of mannes hand so curiously
> Arrayed hadde this gardyn, trewely,
> That nevere was ther gardyn of swich prys,
> But if it were the verray paradis.

Note the artificiality of 'peynted', 'craft' and 'arrayed'; 'curiously' (meaning elaborately or intricately) connects its appearance with the formal arts of courtly behaviour; finally comes the hyperbolic reference to 'paradis', the Garden of

Eden, which, though beautiful, also contained the serpent and unwary human judgement. That the scene takes place in France, the home of courtly love, makes it all the more authentic. Dorigen stands in the garden on the French coast, and sees the black rocks which bar the way to England – where her husband has gone for the stern duty of acquiring honour in war.

The Merchant's Tale

The Merchant's Tale is a much darker narrative because Chaucer parodies *fin amour*. Like *The Franklin's Tale,* it contains husband, wife and young squire, but here their behaviour is selfish and gross. Only the surface gestures and trappings of the noble life remain. Again there is a garden, but by alluding to the beauty of the *hortus conclusus* in *The Song of Solomon* (see Part 1, page 16), Chaucer achieves a grotesque irony. The garden's enclosure is firmly guaranteed by the lustful but blind old man (the *senex amans*), who has a key to lock himself in for sexual sport with his young wife. He is unaware that she has made a copy of the key to give to her young lover, who will hide in the garden and copulate with her in a tree within reach of her blind husband.

Being a young squire, he is the right age for *fin amour*, but he is indelicate in his approach. He becomes the serpent in what is already a false paradise. Chaucer thus subverts the courtly love *topos*, but he could not achieve this so effectively without the three gardens that influenced the genuine *locus amoenus* of poetic convention: *Le Roman de la Rose*, *The Song of Solomon*, the Garden of Eden.

The Pardoner's Tale

A very different type of **iconography** informs *The Pardoner's Tale*. This sinister character, also from *The Canterbury Tales*, tells of three violent young drunkards who burst out of a pub to find and destroy Death, who has killed one of their friends. They meet and abuse an old man who then directs them along a crooked path that leads to an oak tree where Death will be waiting for them. Instead they find a hoard of gold, which makes them forget Death. Then, during their schemes to carry away the gold in secret, they conspire against each other and eventually die in violent suffering.

This compelling story is very sparse in visual description. The landscape is reduced to nothing more than a stile, a crooked path, a grove and the oak tree. Nor is there much description of the four men. There is no chance of our being distracted from the tale's terrifying irony, supported by the meaning (and not the precise look) of the tree. In 1623 John Donne would write:

> We think that Paradise and Calvarie,
> Christ's Crosse and Adam's tree, stood in one place

In the 1390s, Chaucer's audiences too would be reminded of this traditional link. Adam's time in paradise ended when his eating fruit from the tree of knowledge brought evil into the world. Christ redeemed mankind by being crucified on what was often termed 'the tree'. Medieval iconography sometimes placed a skull at the foot of the cross. In *The Pardoner's Tale* the gold that delights the drunkards turns them directly into corpses. The tree being an oak may carry an especially English association; the crooked way to it implies deviousness.

There is great value in Chaucer's simplicity, which seems to withhold meaning and prompts readers and audiences to feel that they have to contribute. In modern times Samuel Beckett gives his stage directions in *Waiting for Godot*: 'A country road. A tree. Evening.' Admittedly, the culture of 1955 is different from Chaucer's in 1390: the meanings of gardens, trees and roads cannot now be assumed on the basis of common culture and reading. Nonetheless, hearing Chaucer's poem and watching Beckett's play seem to put us in touch with something elemental and universal that has its roots in a barely visual response to landscape.

Shakespeare's landscapes

A poem or a novel needs only a reader's imagination for it to communicate, but a play has to travel through the interpretation of a director, designer and actors before it reaches an audience. If the playwright specifies an outdoor scene, today's designer and lighting designer rarely express it naturalistically when they set it in the theatre. Edward Gordon Craig's pioneering work in symbolic and abstract design around 1910 swept aside the typical Victorian and Edwardian visual traditions. Craig and his followers did not aim for detailed authenticity in the historical and **topographical** look of a play's design.

Beerbohm Tree's 1906 production of *A Midsummer Night's Dream* was elaborately old-fashioned. It tried to convince the indoor audience that they were looking at a recognisable English wood (supposedly near Duke Theseus' Athens), with the addition of features that Shakespeare doesn't mention, like believable bushes, trees, grass – even live rabbits. The actual words of the play give just a few details of landscape – notably Oberon's brief but evocative description of Titania's flower-strewn 'bank where the wild thyme blows' – but for characters lost in the wood and lost in their emotional turmoil, it is darkness and fog that predominate. When the script refers to features of the natural world most modern stage designs give them a metaphorical or symbolic value. The director and designer ask an audience to engage with the 'landscape' of the mind more than with a literal wood.

Beneath the surface of nature

Though Shakespeare doesn't give a novelist's close attention to landscape, many of his plays explore concepts of nature, in various aspects ranging from cruel to restorative. In *King Lear* Edmund, with his ruthless and cunning ambition, sees his 'goddess' Nature as a predator. At an opposite extreme in *Pericles*, Lord Cerimon, the healer, knows of all 'the blest infusions / That dwell in vegitives, in metals, stones', and through his art, allied to nature, he can even restore the seeming dead to life. Thus Shakespeare penetrates through the surface of the natural world and explores the almost magical values that lie beneath.

In *The Tempest* (1611) Prospero, a Renaissance scholar, has devoted his life to natural magic. When, in Act 5, he renounces his powers, Shakespeare adapts a description from Ovid's *Metamorphoses* (see Part 1, page 14) where the sorceress Medea enters a night-time landscape. In her incantation, she recalls her dark control over spirits from the hills, trees, woods and streams, all for her purposes of forbidden magic. Prospero's art has thus become dangerous by association with her. In the same play the savage Caliban, himself the child of a witch, complains of Prospero as a ruthless coloniser. Prospero has a power that cannot be resisted, but Caliban has the prior claim to the island, and he speaks of it with a unique love and intuitive knowledge that amount to natural rights of dwelling. He remembers that when Prospero arrived he was subtle in his charms; Caliban's gratitude proved to be naive:

> (thou) wouldst give me
> Water with berries in't, and teach me how
> To name the bigger light and how the less,
> That burn by day and night; and then I loved thee,
> And showed thee all the qualities o'th'isle,
> The fresh springs, brine-pits, barren place and fertile.

Caliban's simple language expresses a deep identification with his territory, later made deeper still by his hearing the strange and potent music of the island. By contrast, some of the 'invading' courtiers are corrupt and manipulative. In this polarity of court and country, Shakespeare continues the traditions of the pastoral (see Part 1, page 23), which had strongly influenced several of his earlier comedies in the 1590s.

A typical comic structure presents a sophisticated court or city that is erratic, misguided or brutal. Dissident courtiers are banished or choose to retire to the country, where honest values, true love and the simple rhythms of nature remove the discord. Those who submit to nature's healing redemption can return in the final act to the court, which is thereby promised a more harmonious future. *The Winter's Tale* exemplifies this pattern. The wintry Sicilian court has become a place of loss, grief and penitence. But, unknown to the suffering characters, 'the red blood reigns in the winter's pale'. Time moves on sixteen years and the predominant influence is spring in Bohemia. The young lovers overcome all threats, comic and serious, and their marriage redeems the errors of the past. Shakespeare acknowledges the subtitle of his source – *The Triumph of Time*, with Nature as Time's partner.

As You Like It

As You Like It owes more than any other comedy to the idealised pastoral tradition. But many other views of the land go to influence this fascinating and complex play. It pretends to be set in France, but Shakespeare translates Ardennes into the Forest of Arden, closely associated with the very English Sherwood Forest of Robin Hood (see Part 1, page 20) and the Arden of his native Warwickshire (from which Shakespeare's mother, Mary Arden derived her family name). Several characters refer to a dead hero, Sir Rowland de Boys (or Bois, meaning wood) whose second son, Orlando, undergoes a pastoral education to become the young hero for the new generation.

The exiled lords, mutually loyal, hunt in the greenwood. They variously value, sympathise with, kill and eat the deer and sing songs around the fire as they feast. This exclusively male group allows Shakespeare to merge the English tradition of Robin Hood with the ancient pastoral of shepherds in love, the classically named Silvius and Phebe. Orlando plays his part in both groups and the heroine Rosalind observes the lovers; her participation takes their traditionally frustrated love-laments into a series of challenging debates. Her quick mind and lively emotions lead her, like the play as a whole, to both idealism and irony. Her wit, that of the jester Touchstone and the would-be jester Jaques lead to a wide-ranging critique of idealistic values: faithful love, emotional honesty, male bonding – and even the temperate climate of a pastoral landscape. The exiled Duke has to accept that they all live in a fallen world (see Part 1, page 15) that includes 'the penalty of Adam / The seasons' difference, as the icy fang / And churlish chiding of the winter's wind'.

The play includes other outdoor realities. Corin, the old shepherd, wise in his simplicity, refers to the difficulties of farming, of renting land, of grasping absentee landlords, of an increasing Elizabethan practice to enclose common arable land for sheep and the profitable wool-trade. Though the play begins on a country estate, there is no rural harmony; a violent family quarrel imposes injustice on Orlando and his old servant Adam. Both are evicted. This play, like many other pastorals, uses the form as a mask: under the safety of the pastoral, the play can examine society and make political protest against abuses.

Nature and politics

When powerful men cherish the land, then human society can flourish. Thus in *Richard II* an entire scene between two apparently irrelevant gardeners makes a well-tended garden a metaphor for good order in the state. And in Act 5 of *Henry V*, a play devoted to war and its politics, the Duke of Burgundy speaks of 'this best garden of the world, / Our fertile France'. He finds virtue not in a natural wilderness, but in skilfully harmonising human art with nature's gifts. The male values of war have devastated the female countryside. Peace and France, both personified as women, are victims, and Burgundy, pleading for a new 'garden'-based civilisation, deplores the neglected landscape:

> Her vine, the merry cheerer of the heart,
> Unpruned dies; her hedges even-pleach'd
> Like prisoners wildly overgrown with hair,
> Put forth disorder'd twigs; her fallow leas
> The darnel, hemlock and rank fumitory
> Doth root upon, while that the coulter rusts
> That should deracinate such savagery;
> The even mead, that erst brought sweetly forth
> The freckled cowslip, burnet and green clover,
> Wanting the scythe, all uncorrected, rank,
> Conceives by idleness, and nothing teems
> But hateful docks, rough thistles, kecksies, burrs,
> Losing both beauty and utility.

This is a view coloured by nostalgia, but it is also very practical: 'beauty and utility' are not opposites, as they might be in the Romantic era (see Part 3, page 90).

Wherever his plays are notionally set, Shakespeare's imaginative sense of dwelling feels local to Warwickshire, where he was born and where he often returned from his work in London. His sense of being English is both less and more than nationalism: it works on and from the small scale, and by depending on his detailed observation of local customs, dialects, plants and landscape, it becomes more powerfully rooted than political theory could on its own.

Marvell's ingenuity

Andrew Marvell (1621–1678) is a 'green' poet, but not in our sense of ecology and conservation. For him 'green' includes growth, nature's profusion, the primitive world and a type of contemplation that even becomes mystical. 'The Garden' (1652) describes the poet's mental journey away from 'the busie Companies of Men', away too from the traditional values of human love, towards the luxury of nature seducing him with gifts. Then the sixth verse departs from this playful, even satirical, process, and creates a still new world for the contemplative pilgrim:

> Mean while the Mind, from pleasure less,
> Withdraws into its happiness:
> The mind, that Ocean where each kind
> Does straight its own resemblance find;
> Yet it creates, transcending these,
> Far other Worlds, and other Seas;
> Annihilating all that's made
> To a green Thought in a green shade.

The abstract sense that suddenly enters the poem in this verse owes something to Plato's theory of forms and also to a medieval view that everything on earth finds its ideal counterpart in the mystery of the ocean. For Marvell the mind responds to what it finds on its journey away from the public world, through the experience of two lovers to contemplative Adam, the first man in solitude. But, more than this, the mind has creative powers too in its own mystical world that is twice green: the literal shady refuge from business (or 'busy-ness'); then the generative thought, that leads on to the Soul, poised bird-like in the branches, and 'prepar'd for longer flight'.

Critics have plundered this extraordinary poem for its allusions to theology and philosophy, not to mention the Garden of Eden and lovers from Ovid's *Metamorphoses*. Under the weight of this apparatus it is easy to lose track of how nimble Marvell is. He is teasingly circular too: the first lines refer to men struggling for high achievement and fame; at the end it is 'th'industrious bee' that 'Computes its time as well as we', but under a 'milder Sun' that ensures that a better regulated time passes under nature's benign authority.

Adapting the pastoral

Marvell adapts the pastoral convention in other ways too. In the 'Mower' poems Damon is obsessed by Juliana and suffers the heat of unfulfilled love under a hot July sun. But his scythe, slicing the green grass, indicates a fallen world of time passing, violence and imminent death. Even the poem of tribute, 'The Picture of little T.C. in a Prospect of Flowers', ends with an anxiety about premature death as he urges the girl to 'Gather the Flow'rs, but spare the Buds.' Marvell's real-life experience as tutor to a prosperous family gives a new twist to the role of poet as pastoral lover: he is an adult educating a child about the world, but he is also below her in social status. And, being a child, she is also closer to nature than he, the bookish tutor:

> In the green Grass she loves to lie,
> And there with her fair Aspect tames
> The Wilder flow'rs, and gives them names

Marvell privileges childhood in ways that bring him close to Wordsworth (see page 60, below), though in more playfully inventive ways. In 1653 he became tutor to Lord Fairfax's daughter, Maria, at the family's country house. Fairfax, soldier and statesman, served under Cromwell, and, like him, retired from London to the country for periods of reflective life. Marvell's longest poem, 'Upon Appleton House' (1652), is another poem of tribute – to the family and its history as well as to the house and its landscape. But he tempers this serious purpose with amusing fantasy, like a metaphysical Lewis Carroll. This is his impression of the flowers at night:

> But when the vigilant Patroul
> Of Stars walks round about the Pole,

Their leaves, that to the stalks are curl'd,
Seem to their Staves the Ensigns furl'd.
Then in some Flow'rs beloved Hut
Each Bee as Sentinel is shut;
And sleeps so too: but, if once stirr'd,
She runs you through, nor askes the Word.

Later he develops conceits that the meadows are seas, that grasshoppers are giants in the world of grass, that he is 'an inverted tree'; the oaks stoop down to hear the nightingale, boats sail over bridges, fish are found in the stable. 'Strange Prophecies my Phancy weaves' – a result of his reading in 'Nature's mystick Book'. The fantastical world stops to admire when Maria steps out, but the poet's inventive mind doesn't stop working. Even the sunset becomes an ingenious tribute:

The Sun himself, of Her aware,
Seems to descend with greater care;
And lest she see him go to Bed,
In blushing Clouds conceals his Head.

Like Little T.C., she has lineage, beauty, virtue, power over men, a high destiny and the poet combines with nature to worship her.

As with Chaucer, Marvell enjoys his self-deprecating persona. He makes himself a passive object for seduction, but it is nature, not a woman, who ravishes him. In the fifth verse of 'The Garden' the fruits and flowers give him a 'wond'rous life': 'The Luscious Clusters of the Vine / Upon my Mouth do crush their Wine'. In 'Upon Appleton House' he passes from the house, through the garden and meadows to the dark forest, where again seduction awaits him.

In 'Bermudas' (1653) he recalls an emigration voyage by Puritans in 1635 and uses it to imagine sailing from a corrupted England 'Unto an Isle so long unknown', a primitive past with connotations of the Garden of Eden. They enjoy figs, melons and apples; they have arrived at the 'grassy stage' on which God as landscape-designer 'hangs in shades the Orange bright, / Like golden Lamps in a green Night'.

'The Coronet'

The pastoral poet is bound to be self-conscious in deploying his art. In Marvell's day this would not be cause for criticism – nor should it in ours. But 'The Coronet' (pub. 1681) takes self-consciousness a stage further. It is a poem about writing poems and the skilful poet's motivation in displaying his craft. As a pastoral love poet he has created garlands (of words) to celebrate his girl-friend as a fictitious shepherdess. His ingenious wit has been so elaborate that the garlands for her head are better described as 'fragrant towers'. But should such gifts be offered to a woman, when, as an ordinary sinful man, the poet owes more in penitence to his God? He must abandon love poetry and write his tribute instead to Christ, who, in suffering for mankind, wears his own garland, the crown of thorns. The impulsive poet decides to surpass himself, and other poets too:

> So rich a Chaplet thence to weave
> As never yet the king of Glory wore.

Then suddenly he catches himself being too devoted to 'Fame and (self-)Interest'. Vanity, his motive, like 'the Serpent old', quietly alongside mankind since the Garden of Eden, has disguised itself among the flowers of rhetoric. As serpent-motive, it weaves insidiously like the syntax of a poem, like the poet's complicated wit. It has become a 'winding snare' and must be destroyed. The poet must sacrifice the skill that has given him pleasure and self-esteem; he has to accept that his flowers must 'wither',

> Though set with Skill and chosen out with Care.

He allows himself this last moment of regret before making the final sacrifice: Christ will tread on the spoils of his art, so that the coronet 'May crown thy Feet, that could not crown thy Head.'

'The Coronet' cannot help being a witty and graceful piece, almost contradicting its austere message. In syntax and poetic form it feels like a carefully woven garland (or 'tower', 'chaplet', 'wreath', 'diadem', 'coronet' or 'crown'). It is circular too, beginning with the crown of thorns and ending with the crucified Saviour's feet, which, when visualised, are seen to have been raised to the level of a head that can be crowned. The poem skilfully links nature (from the traditional pastoral), and moves, through half-reluctant penitence and consummate art, to the grace of God.

Landscapes for elegy

In Old English literature the word 'elegy' denoted a poem that meditated on the transience of the world. In Renaissance times an elegy might be, more generally, a reflective poem. Later the term came to be used in the modern sense of a poem of mourning. Matthew Arnold's 'Thyrsis' (1866) commemorates Arthur Clough, a close friend and fellow-poet, and in 1875 Hopkins wrote 'The Wreck of the Deutschland' to mourn a group of drowned nuns, not known to the poet.

Many elegies have a pastoral setting, because solitude in nature allows the poet to reflect on what has been lost. Also, if nature is personified and shares in the poet's grief, it seems more genuine and permanent than the busy world, which keeps moving on and has less time and heart to spend on commemoration.

Chaucer: *The Book of the Duchess*

The Book of the Duchess (1369) was one of Chaucer's very early works, in which he skilfully adapted the French courtly love convention of the dream poem for the purpose of elegy. Chaucer wrote this elegy to be read at court in the presence of John of Gaunt, Duke of Lancaster, whose wife, Lady Blanche, had died in an outbreak of plague. In a dream the narrator goes hunting, is separated from the group and wanders into a forest where he meets a dejected young knight, dressed in black. The knight trusts the sympathetic narrator enough to celebrate his lady's unique beauty and virtue, and to speak of his loss.

Chaucer gives his brief description of the dream's setting a social and psychological **decorum**. There is a fresh, active spring morning for the aristocratic hunt and the contrasting dark forest for the knight's solitude. The 'hart' seems to elude the hunters, just as the secrets of the knight's 'heart' need to be coaxed from the depths of his suffering. The narrator fails to keep up with the hunt because he is incompetent, but the knight chooses to be alone to grieve. The improbable situation of a humble, self-effacing poet acting almost as counsellor to the greatest nobleman is softened firstly by the distancing effect of the dream, and then by the strange recession (as in the nave of a gothic cathedral) of penetrating deep into the forest. As with Keats' sonnet mentioned in the Introduction (page 6), the forest symbolises the depths of the brain or spirit, which is more profound than the mere social distinctions of real life.

Milton: *Lycidas*

Milton's *Lycidas* (1637) is much shorter – just 193 lines – but is packed with detail from the poet's reading and observation. Critics have praised it as one of the greatest pastoral elegies: for Henry King, Milton's friend and fellow-poet from Cambridge, who drowned at sea. Dr Johnson disagreed, believing that its literary artifice prevented the expression of personal grief. But Johnson couldn't accept that Milton aimed to be more public than personal. He was commemorating a talent prematurely destroyed; his poem made a statement, much as a sculpture may in a public square. He hoped that his elegy would perpetuate King's fame and also Milton's own beliefs about the state of the contemporary Church.

Read in this way, the elegy benefits from artifice and convention: Milton and King are, as it were, fellow-shepherds training to care for their flock (in other words, their parishioners if and when they take holy orders); the poet begs major and minor gods to share in the grief, as nature already does:

> Thee Shepherd, thee the Woods, and desert caves,
> With wilde Thyme and the gadding vine o'regrown,
> And all their echoes mourn.

Later he contrasts the frightening seas 'where ere thy bones are hurl'd' with the relatively slight gestures that the river god can ask nature to give. This takes the form of a catalogue of flowers, borrowed perhaps from Spenser and Shakespeare, but written with a formal grace rather than the vividness of real life:

> The Musk-rose, and the well-attir'd Woodbine,
> With Cowslips wan that hang the pensive head,
> And every flower that sad embroidery wears.

Milton concludes with far more optimism than appears in the *Book of the Duchess*, where Chaucer awakes puzzled but determined to make a poem from his dream. Milton imagines a glorious new life for Lycidas, recognises that his commemorative task is over and moves on to the next stage of his own life, evoking both dusk and dawn (for reflection and then new literary achievement):

> And now the Sun had stretch'd out all the hills,
> And now was dropt into the Western bay;
> At last he rose, and twitch'd his Mantle blue:
> Tomorrow to fresh Woods, and pastures new.

Elegies for the poor and those who died in war

Both elegies considered above commemorate young people who possessed high status or special talent; the world in general (as well as those close to them) suffered from their premature death. But elegies may also be written for those who were poor or disregarded. Their sad anonymity sometimes produces a special pathos.

In 1750 Thomas Gray wrote his now-famous 'Elegy Written in a Country Churchyard'. The setting is amongst the graves; from there the poet reaches out to the traditional landscape of rural life, and reflects on fame and simple integrity. In Wordsworth's 'The Ruined Cottage' (1797) there is more focus on an individual. A pedlar tells the poet the story of Margaret who pines away for her soldier-husband. There is an implied social message here about the suffering of the very poor: they are denied even the sense of community described by Gray in his gentler landscape. Wordsworth's almost ruthless detail in describing the neglect of the cottage and its garden contribute to the utter bleakness of this elegy.

War, and especially civil war, calls for commemoration of the dead and their connection to the land that nurtured them. In his 'Drummer Hodge' (1899) Hardy celebrates an ordinary man from the west country who died far from home in the Boer War; Housman's 'A Shropshire Lad' (1896), a collection of lyrics, wistfully evokes familiar countryside for men going off to war. Seamus Heaney's *Field Work* (1979) includes several elegies to young men murdered in the Irish conflicts; 'The Strand at Lough Beg' contrasts the terrifying road block, 'voices, heads hooded and the cold nosed gun' with the calm strand where 'the cattle graze / Up to their bellies in an early mist'.

There are even elegies by poets speculating about their own deaths and what should be said of them, when they are not there to find the words. In his sonnet 'If I should die …' [in battle] (pub. 1916) Rupert Brooke foretells that, in him, part of the English landscape will reside in France. In 'Afterwards' (1917) Hardy hopes that he will be remembered as a reflective man able to respond sensitively to nature.

Landscapes for religion

In the visual arts of the Renaissance it was rare (at least in oil paintings and frescoes) for landscapes to appear without a human subject. Artists gave appropriate, and often symbolic, landscape settings to support their stories of Christ and the saints. In his book, *Landscape and Western Art* (1999), Malcolm Andrews gives special attention to versions of St Jerome's penance in the wilderness: some develop an impression of narrative by showing the city which he left behind; some concentrate on the wilderness as a place of savagery and demons. Those that, more optimistically, show the landscape miraculously reviving as a result of holy prayers were beginning to merge two traditions of depicting the world beyond the city walls: the classical rural retreat deriving from Virgil's *Georgics* (see Part 1, page 12), and the more austere Christian belief in solitude to refresh the world-wearied soul.

Devotional writing also uses landscape, especially where the Christian life is expressed allegorically in the form of a journey. Bunyan's *Pilgrim's Progress* (1678) describes Christian's journey to the Celestial City. He faces hazards in places such as the Slough of Despond, the Valley of Humiliation and the Hill of Difficulty. There are more pleasant experiences too: Immanuel's Land, his meeting with shepherds on the Delectable Mountains.

Milton: *Paradise Lost*

Milton's *Paradise Lost* (1667) was almost contemporary with Bunyan's allegory, but he was writing on a vast scale: an epic poem to 'justify the ways of God to men'. Milton invents a terrifying landscape for hell, and a calm and fertile state of perfection for Adam and Eve in the Garden of Eden (see Part 3, page 88). He depicts a complex relationship between man and nature: in Book 4, he describes the bower, a place not constructed (like Satan's Pandaemonium) but composed of trees and flowers woven together naturally and growing from the earth. By dwelling in Eden, Adam and Eve are rooted in their environment. In this, Milton is rejecting a medieval distinction between the pure soul destined for heaven and the physical senses which belong to the contaminating world.

Eve, especially, is identified with flowers; she is part of 'mother' Earth (see Part 4, page 106). When she takes the forbidden fruit she does more than disobey God; she aspires to a type of knowledge that is sudden and disconnected from the life she was created into. She uproots her natural dwelling with the earth, she eats, 'And highth'nd as with Wine', she worships the tree as if it were a god outside herself. The archangel Raphael had promised Adam that, after 'long obedience tri'd', there would be no longer any distinction between heaven and earth. But this would depend on Adam's waiting for the appointed season and on not breaking the natural process and rhythm of life in the garden under God.

The consequence of Adam and Eve's sin is that they lose their dwelling-place and must wander. The last lines of the poem may seem initially to imply a type of freedom:

> The world was all before them, where to choose
> Their place of rest, and providence their guide:
> They hand in hand with wand'ring steps and slow,
> Through Eden took their solitary way.

But they know that their new space is in fact imprisonment. The rhythms of the language reinforce the sense of loss: 'a place of rest' somewhere is not the same as dwelling in their own place, and without Eden they must be 'solitary'. The suffering is reciprocal: when Eve sinned 'Earth felt the wound', perhaps reminding readers that she was born from a rib pulled from Adam's side. When he eats, 'Earth trembl'd from her entrails', a parody and reversal of childbirth. The garden suffers to let them go; they suffer in leaving it.

In Milton's lifetime the English countryside was suffering. In particular, ancient forests were being destroyed for ships, smelting and for many other types of industry and building. In 1664 the diarist John Evelyn wrote *Silva*, urging government action to preserve the forests. In the Victorian era industry was even more widespread and the countryside more devastated; another religious poet Gerard Manley Hopkins (1844–1889) protested, in 'Binsey Poplars' (1879), about the destruction of trees.

Hopkins

For Hopkins nature was sacramental, though as a young man training to be a Jesuit priest, he was scrupulously self-denying and halted his creative writing, because he feared that love of poetry might be a self-indulgence and love of nature might distract him from God. His superior priest at the seminary in Wales persuaded him that his gifts were God-given and that he should respond as a poet (as well as a priest) to a disaster in 1875, when a group of German nuns, emigrating for a new life in America, were drowned in a shipwreck. His greatest poem, 'The Wreck of the Deutschland' explores God's providence in so wantonly (as it seemed) destroying the innocent. He describes himself 'on a pastoral forehead of Wales' responding to the event and he sees God in the stars and the sunset:

> I kiss my hand
> To the stars, lovely asunder
> Starlight, wafting him out of it; and
> Glow, glory in thunder;
> Kiss my hand to the dappled-with-damson west

His descriptions of nature are rarely static: either he writes with a restrained energy, as here, or, as with most of the poem, his powerful verbs catch a sense of divine 'instress'. Hopkins derived this word from the Greek philosopher Parmenides and applied it in his own Christian awareness of God's energy working within the whole of the created world. An example is his extraordinarily dense language to describe a snowstorm, full of compounds and alliteration: 'Wiry and white-fiery and whirlwind-swivelled snow.' The meaning of 'instress' often overlaps with 'inscape' (see page 71, below).

In gentler but exuberant mood Hopkins wrote 'The May Magnificat' (1878), connecting spring with Mary's glorifying the Lord. As spring comes each year, so our worship should be constant and recurrent, seeing Christ's birth reflected in the season's new life:

> When drop-of-blood-and-foam-dapple
> Bloom lights the orchard-apple
>   And thicket and thorp are merry
>   With silver-surfèd cherry
>
> And azuring-over greybell makes
> Wood-banks and brakes wash wet like lake.
>   And magic cuckoocall
>   Caps, clears, and clinches all –
>
> This ecstasy all through mothering earth
> Tells Mary her mirth till Christ's birth
>   To remember and exultation
>   In God who was her salvation.

▶ Consider how Hopkins combines worship of God with his response to nature. Compare these verses with his sonnet 'Spring' (Part 3, page 87).

T.S. Eliot

Hopkins sees and hears the created world around him and worships God through his experiences of nature. In spite of this devout certainty (at least in his early poems), he was criticised for being obscure as he tried to find new ways with words to convey what his senses told him. Fifty years later, the Anglo-Catholic poet T.S. Eliot (1888–1965) was obscure in different and more intellectual ways. His poems search for stability; they are not about discovery, nor the intensity of committed worship. Not only was he living in a world that felt fragmented, he was also exploring the possibilities of language, and especially its music and half-perceived associations, and making, as he put it, 'raids on the inarticulate'.

Eliot's two greatest poems *The Waste Land* (1922) and *Four Quartets* (1935–1942) are not organic, they are sometimes barely coherent, and often abandon normal logic. A first reading is likely to reach the understanding more through sound and intermittent glimpses than through conceptual meaning:

> For most of us, there is only the unattended
> Moment, the moment in and out of time,
> The distraction fit, lost in a shaft of sunlight,
> The wild thyme unseen, or the winter lightning
> Or the waterfall, or music heard so deeply
> That it is not heard at all.

These lines from *The Dry Salvages* (the third of *Four Quartets*) may seem to describe the process of reading Eliot as much as Eliot's own search for his inner stability.

The Waste Land is a bleak poem, communicating through 'a heap of broken images', focusing largely on the 'unreal' city, but using basic images from the landscape beyond, such as rocks, water, arid plains, distant mountains, wind crossing the brown land. Eliot draws on fragments of received culture, from literary, Christian and eastern religions, merging them with glimpses of deadened or emptily vigorous contemporary life. The poem's ironic opening parodies the first lines of *The Canterbury Tales* in which Chaucer describes the energy of new spring life; Eliot starts with spring in order to question its creative force:

> April is the cruellest month, breeding
> Lilacs out of the dead land, mixing
> Memory and desire, stirring
> Dull roots with spring rain.

Four Quartets is more varied in evoking nature. Each poem opens with a sense of place and each takes its title from a particular place: Burnt Norton is a Gloucestershire manor house; East Coker in Somerset was the home of the Eliot family before they emigrated to New England; the Dry Salvages are rocks off the New England coast; Little Gidding is an Anglican shrine and home to a religious community. All, therefore, are personal to Eliot and are quiet, private places suitable for meditation, especially on the relationship between time, place and the contemplative mind that tries to work through paradox towards resolved meaning. *Little Gidding*, the last of the *Quartets*, opens with a journey (see Part 3, page 98) towards the shrine where the poet reflects:

> The moment of the rose and the moment of the yew-tree
> Are of equal duration. A people without history
> Is not redeemed from time, for history is a pattern
> Of timeless moments. So, while the light fails
> On a winter's afternoon, in a secluded chapel
> History is now and England.

The country house

The country house poem was a familiar genre in hierarchical English society. The poet pays tribute to the noble lord with his pen, while the tenants offer their rural produce and skills. Respect is based on tradition and continuity. The productivity of the land is matched by the family, stretching back through the centuries and continuing to produce noble heirs who will maintain their rank and integrity; they should recognise too that privilege brings responsibilities towards the tenants and to the estate. Poems that celebrate these values, that are both local and English, have little concern for the land's aesthetic appeal; substance matters far more than surface.

Nature tamed for productivity

In 'Penshurst' (1616) Ben Jonson celebrates the country estate owned by Sir Philip Sidney's family; the house is not built for modern effects of 'envious show', but is an 'ancient pile' attracting even the classical gods Pan and Bacchus, as well as 'ruddy satyres' and 'The lighter fauns'. Social distinctions matter, but have no effect on the welcome of guests: 'all come in, the farmer and the clowne', the poet relaxes as if 'I reigned here', and when King James arrives unexpectedly the house is ready to entertain him.

Jonson gives little topographical detail: the visual effect is of tasteful restraint, whereas the emphasis on soil, air, wood and water leads to a hyperbole of dense productivity:

> The lower land, that to the river bends,
> Thy sheep, thy bullocks, kine, and calves do feed:
> The middle grounds thy mares, and horses breed.
> Each banke doth yeeld thee coneyes

Fish, game and fruit are not simply prolific: they offer themselves up and beg to be eaten. The poem is written partly to celebrate virtue, partly to condemn superficiality:

> Now, Penshurst, they that will proportion thee
> With other edifices, when they see
> Those proud ambitious heaps, and nothing else,
> May say, their lords have built, but thy lord dwells.

'Dwells' is the poem's last word: there is a distinction between a lord who builds, owns and lives in a *house*, and a *home* where a nobleman dwells and benefits the whole community.

Following Jonson's example, the metaphysical poet Thomas Carew (1594–1640) celebrated another country house, 'Saxham' (pub. 1640), in similar, if more playful, terms: fertility of the land, hospitality, respect from the neighbours. He cannot see the landscape properly because, when he arrives in winter, frost and snow conceal its beauties, but he gracefully feels that winter cannot detract, nor spring add, any delights. The important values are permanent and are not those of superficial aesthetics.

Alexander Pope celebrated virtue, but built his reputation on brilliant satire. In his Moral Epistle 'On The Use of Riches' (1731–1735) he attacks empty grandeur in the character of 'Timon'; he uses visual effects to mock Timon and his values:

> Greatness, with Timon, dwells in such a draught
> As brings all Brobdignag before your thought.
> To compass this, his building is a town,
> His pond an ocean, his parterre a down:
> Who but must laugh, the master when he sees,
> A puny insect, shivering at a breeze!
> Lo, what huge heaps of littleness around!
> The whole, a labour'd quarry above ground,
> Two cupids squirt before: a lake behind
> Improves the keenness of the northern wind.

▶ How does Pope achieve his satirical effect in these lines? Consider surprise, irony, the relationship of people to landscape and the varied rhythms within the **heroic couplets**.

The aesthetic effect: the house and its estate

Jane Austen is not especially noted for writing long stretches of landscape description. When she does (see Part 3, page 90), she generally implies social and moral judgements. Such judgements also arise in Chapter 43 of *Pride and Prejudice*. Elizabeth Bennett is touring in Derbyshire with her aunt and uncle; they visit Pemberley, the home of Mr Darcy whose proposal of marriage Elizabeth has not just rejected, but firmly snubbed. Without her own hasty prejudice (and some pride), she could have been mistress of this house and its vast estate.

> ... the eye was instantly caught by Pemberley House, situated on the opposite side of the valley, into which the road with some abruptness wound. It was a large, handsome, stone building, standing well on rising ground, and backed by a ridge of high woody hills; – and in front, a stream of some natural importance was swelled into greater, but without any artificial appearance. Its banks were neither formal, nor falsely adorned. Elizabeth was delighted. She had never seen a place for which nature had done more, or where natural beauty had been so little counteracted by an awkward taste.

Elizabeth is sometimes inclined to be sharply critical and certainly prejudiced against Darcy, but here she admires his good taste. She is on holiday to enjoy picturesque scenes and she picks on the relationship of wood, water, hill and house, with attention to natural curves in the landscape rather than formal symmetry. Human judgement and money have respected nature and cooperated with the 'genius of the place' (see Part 1, page 27). When the group is shown round the house, they find the same tact and balance within as outside in the grounds.

'Standing well on rising ground', the house announces authority. But Darcy is not given to grandeur or vanity; he knows the responsibilities of his social position and he has a natural grace, the respect and affection of his subordinates and is very attentive to guests. He ensures that Mr Gardiner enjoys his fishing on the river, a sedate and middle-class equivalent of an aristocrat's hunting.

Austen published her novel in 1813. The modern playwright Tom Stoppard set his *Arcadia* (1993) in a Derbyshire country house in 1809. Elizabeth Bennett was looking for the picturesque partly as a refreshing change from her more pastoral home in Hertfordshire; Stoppard's title helps to show how the fashion for the serene pastoral was being challenged by the new taste for picturesque, verging on the gothic. Noakes, the landscape gardener in Arcadia, is having a tough time. He is challenged by a robust traditionalist: 'Is Sidley Park to be an Englishman's garden or the haunt of Corsican brigands?' Even his employer Lady Croom is entertainingly outraged:

> My hyacinth dell is become a haunt for hobgoblins, my Chinese bridge, which I am assured is superior to the one at Kew, and for all I know at Peking, is usurped by a fallen obelisk overgrown with briars.

Landscape is a witty adjunct to the play and contributes to its major theme: the way Enlightenment reason was being taken over by the new cult of feeling, so that it was possible for chaos to be interpreted as genius.

The country house disturbed

Pride and Prejudice ends happily as Elizabeth's married life begins at Pemberley. However, some novels based on life in a country house and its grounds tell disturbing stories, and landscape description contributes to unease. L.P. Hartley's *The Go-Between* (1953) and Ian McEwan's *Atonement* (2001) are both set in large old houses where the resident family has to deal with social disparity. Marian Maudesley and Cecilia Tallis both fall in love with young men from the working class, respectively a farmer and a gardener; Cecilia's case is complicated by the fact that both she and Robbie are bright Oxford undergraduates reading English Literature.

Hartley makes much of the relentless heat and the sinister growths round the shady outhouses; he links the state of nature with the story's placing in 1900, the turning point that signifies social change. McEwan describes the driveway and, especially, the fountain in ways that both evoke the timeless security that the house in its landscape should provide, but which also undermine the potential idyll with social and aesthetic dislocation. He achieves most of this through the viewpoint of Briony, the precocious and disturbed thirteen year-old. The night-time scene that leads immediately to her crucial false evidence depends on the landscape, normally familiar, having a weirdly disorientating effect on her:

> The building's indistinct pallor shimmered in the dark. When she stared at it directly it dissolved completely. It stood about a hundred feet away, and nearer, in the grassy stretch, there was a shrub she did not remember. Or rather, she remembered it being closer to the shore. The trees were not right either, what she could see of them. The oak was too bulbous, the elm too straggly, and in their strangeness they seemed in league. As she put her hand out to touch the parapet of the bridge, a duck startled her with a high, unpleasant call, almost human in its breathy downward note.

▶ There are excellent films of *Pride and Prejudice, The Go-Between* and *Atonement*. Compare their treatments of landscape with the authors' descriptions in the novels. How do these visual contexts contribute to each novel's atmosphere and the feelings of the characters?

Romantic solitude

Emily Brontë (1818–1848) is best known for her novel *Wuthering Heights* (1846) with its solitary hero, Heathcliff. She was also a passionate poet:

> I'll walk where my own nature would be leading:
> It vexes me to choose another guide:
> Where the grey flocks in ferny glades are feeding;
> Where the wild wind blows on the mountainside.

These lines from her 'Always rebuked ...' (1839) show a solitary independence at home among northern hills and fells. 'Wild' describes landscape and is also, by extension, a powerful trait in a Romantic poet.

In 'Tintern Abbey' (1798) Wordsworth returns to a place by the River Wye which had sustained him spiritually five years earlier. First he hears the 'waters rolling from their mountain-springs', then he sees

> steep and lofty cliffs,
> That on a wild secluded scene impress
> Thoughts of more deep seclusion.

'Wild' landscape and the poet's 'seclusion' together produce intense feeling. Though the poem begins with green wildness near 'pastoral farms', it is not so much about landscape as about its effect on the poet's inner state. For 110 lines he seems to be alone, recalling the past and responding more maturely in his now-five-year-older self. Then he addresses his sister Dorothy, present with him and reacting as he did on his first visit. In her constant support for him she was gentle and self-effacing, but here he values her for something more intense: 'the shooting lights / Of thy wild eyes'. He assures her that being alone and responding deeply to nature will give moral and spiritual strength to face the dreariness of social daily life:

> Therefore let the moon
> Shine on thee in thy solitary walk;
> And let the misty mountain-winds be free
> To blow against thee

Solitude can activate the imagination, stimulate dreams and invite experiences that are more intense and remote than are possible in company. Wordsworth believed that 'The world [in other words, worldliness] is too much with us'. At the end of his sonnet that begins with these words, he wishes for 'glimpses that would make me less forlorn', of mythical gods rising from the sea. The poem has described a type of retreat: from the world of 'getting and spending'; to the poet isolating himself on 'this pleasant lea'; and from this solitude he may see visions.

'The Solitary Reaper' (1807) tells of Wordsworth walking on a hillside and pausing to see a girl working in the fields. Hearing her song, the poet wonders about its subject, whether far-off or 'familiar matter of today'. The valley becomes 'profound' in two senses: it is literally deep and the music allows it to reach beyond itself in time and place. The poem's imaginative value depends on the interaction of landscape, solitude and music. Although he begins by asking us to 'behold' the girl, the poem is really about what he hears: she is simply a channel for the music and what it may evoke. The poet walks on and 'hears' her song 'long after it was heard no more'.

Many critics have commented on the spirituality of the great Romantic poets, not in the sense of organised religion, but in the intensely receptive private visions that grow in solitude, like those of medieval mystics. However, the great difference is that nature is receiving the poets' worship in a form of **pantheism**. God ministers to them through his created world and not through self-denial.

'Ministry', suggesting holiness, is appropriate for Coleridge's intuitions in the first line of 'Frost at Midnight' (1798): 'The frost performs its secret ministry'. Frost comes at night, mysteriously, while the poet sits by a fading fire with his sleeping child. Though the poem is about education (negative for him when young, positive for his child), its title refers to the conditions for meditation. Coleridge, like his friend Wordsworth, is fascinated by the processes of the mind:

> The inmates of my cottage, all at rest,
> Have left me to that solitude, which suits
> Abstruser musings

He feels almost disconcerted by the strange atmosphere. This is such a powerful influence that at the end, after moving rapidly through the seasons, he returns to winter and the poem slows down, back into the stillness of the opening mystery:

> Whether the eve-drops fall
> Heard only in the trances of the blast,
> Or if the secret ministry of frost
> Shall hang them up in silent icicles,
> Quietly shining to the quiet Moon.

Several of the great Romantic poets were intellectually distinguished. Among those who studied at Cambridge, Wordsworth was a mathematician at St John's College; Byron was at Trinity; Coleridge was at Jesus College, and was later recognised as one of the greatest minds of his generation. But they didn't expect scholarship to bring enlightenment; sometimes they disparaged it. As post-Enlightenment poets they looked for wisdom elsewhere.

Matthew Arnold (1822–1888; son of the great headmaster of Rugby and himself Professor of Poetry at Oxford) was a mid-Victorian Romantic. In 1853 he wrote 'The Scholar-Gipsy' to reflect on an old story of an Oxford scholar who abandoned the chance of a conventional career in search of wisdom that is deeper than books could offer. He adopted a gipsy (or drop-out) way of life because solitude in nature was more enriching than both studying alone in libraries and the worldly success that would normally follow. His former friends tried to locate him, but he was always elusive. Arnold drew on his own memories of happy times at university and in the surrounding countryside. For him those times are past, and so the memory invests the poem with melancholy nostalgia, which became a popular feeling in Victorian poetry.

▶ You will find four verses from this poem in Part 3 (page 92). How does Arnold achieve a sense of mystery and melancholy in these lines?

Landscapes of childhood

We could never have loved the earth so well if we had had no childhood in it – if it were not the earth where the same flowers come up again every spring that we used to gather with our tiny fingers as we sat lisping to ourselves on the grass – the same hips and haws on the autumn hedgerows – the same redbreasts that we used to call 'God's birds,' because they did no harm to the precious crops. What novelty is worth that sweet monotony where everything is known, and *loved* because it is known?

The wood I walk in on this mild May day, with the young yellow-brown foliage of the oaks between me and the blue sky, the white star-flowers and the blue-eyed speedwell and the ground-ivy at my feet – what grove of tropic palms, what strange ferns or splendid broad-petalled blossoms, could ever thrill such deep and delicate fibres within me as this home-scene?

This is a passage from Chapter 5 of George Eliot's *The Mill on the Floss* (1861). The authorial voice, evident here, is strong and frequent throughout the novel. Eliot expounds social and philosophical issues and also pushes her own enthusiastic presence into the story of two children, Tom and Maggie Tulliver, who grow up in Lincolnshire and whose bond is rooted deeply into the landscape around their home at Dorlecote Mill. Eliot here contrasts the ordinary flowers around English oak trees with gaudy foreign plants that are more exotic. She implies that a restless urge for fashion is shallow, compared with the humbler integrity of what is 'loved because it is known'. Eliot admired Wordsworth, who strongly idealised childhood, but in this passage she is closer to John Clare (see page 72, below) who expressed love for his birthplace through close observation. Other Romantics writing, for example, in the gothic or sublime manner, might take the opposite view: they preferred stories filled with violent events and extreme passion above the more tamely familiar experiences. And their landscapes match the stories.

The Mill on the Floss opens with water (see Part 3, page 93), the river Floss and its tributary Ripple, which give their father his livelihood. It ends in tragedy, also by water. Maggie's adolescence includes two love affairs, but the deepest relationship is with her brother; their contrasting temperaments lead to a severe quarrel but they become reconciled moments before they drown together in a great flood that overwhelms both river and land. Maggie had always loved the river with its hypnotic sounds and movement:

… the first thing I ever remember in my life is standing with Tom by the side of the Floss while he held my hand – everything before that is dark to me.

And darkness follows too as they suffer death by water, which, though destructive, has also been a life-giving force and has sustained the landscape of their childhood.

The river flows onwards, symbolising change, but paradoxically it will also remain in its place and outlive human beings. The novel ends with reflections on change and memory, explored, as in the first chapter, in terms of landscape. Eliot asks her readers to remember the two children in 'the days when they had clasped their little hands in love, and roamed the daisied fields together'. But memory can be more complicated than simple nostalgia:

> Nature repairs her ravages – but not all. The uptorn trees are not rooted again; the parted hills are left scarred; if there is new growth, the trees are not the same as the old, and the hills underneath the green vesture bear the marks of the past rending. To the eyes that have dwelt on the past, there is no thorough repair.

Wordsworth and Coleridge

Wordsworth's depiction of childhood landscape is less detailed and more visionary. His long poem *The Prelude* (its first version published in 1798) is a verse autobiography that explores the influences on his life lived closely with nature, that nurtured him as a poet. The shorter version, which Wordsworth reduced to two parts, begins, like Eliot's novel, with water:

> Was it for this
> That one, the fairest of all rivers, loved
> To blend his murmurs with my nurse's song,
> And from his alder shades and rocky falls, sent a voice
> That flowed along my dreams?

The 'voice' of the river tempers 'our human waywardness' and gives an intuition of the deeper calm 'Which Nature breathes among the fields and groves'. Wordsworth was writing at this time in close contact with Coleridge, his fellow-poet. He quotes from Coleridge's 'Frost at Midnight' (included in *Lyrical Ballads* on which they collaborated in 1798) when he writes of his 'sweet birthplace' beside the river Derwent. Coleridge's calm childhood was followed by dull, restrictive schooldays, and in the poem he predicts a very different and 'Wordsworthian' education for his own child:

> But thou, my babe! shalt wander like a breeze
> By lakes and sandy shores, beneath the crags
> Of ancient mountain, and beneath the clouds,
> Which image in their bulk both lakes and shores
> And mountain crags: so shalt thou see and hear
> The lovely shapes and sounds intelligible

Of that eternal language, which thy God
Utters, who from eternity doth teach
Himself in all, and all things in himself.

These lines are typical of both poets in their sense of childhood freedom and their placing the small child alongside the massive forces of nature. Both poets feel that God speaks a special 'language' through what he has created, and that nature has the power to educate, though not in any formal or didactic way.

Both poets believed that children are born with the special privilege of deep identification with the natural world around them; this includes fresh and detailed observation, but also extends into spiritual awareness. In his 'Ode: Intimations of Immortality' (1802) Wordsworth believes that 'Our birth is but a sleep and a forgetting', that the young child is closest to 'God, who is our home:', and that becoming an adult and even becoming civilised (which Enlightenment thinkers would value) is really a regression from the most profound experiences and truths. Both poets were influenced by Rousseau (see Part 1, page 31), whose praise for 'primitive' cultures over the 'civilised' is akin to Wordsworth's distinction between the child and the adult. Both the 'savage' and the child live in close contact with nature, and are not contaminated by cities, which diminish sensitive perception and cause moral decline.

Dylan Thomas

'The Cult of Childhood', as the critic Peter Quennell has called it, existed in some form long before 1800, in the visionary 17th-century poets Henry Vaughan and Thomas Traherne. It has extended up to the present day, as a powerful strand of the Romantic movement, and is particularly evident in Irish and Welsh writing. Perhaps the infancy of the British Isles, in these pre-Roman Celtic cultures, is appropriate for the celebration of a child's vision. Dylan Thomas (1914–1953) was too wayward to share Wordsworth's high philosophical vision, but his poem 'Fern Hill' (1946) experiments more boldly with the half-surreal way in which a child may view the nature around him:

Now as I was young and easy under the apple boughs
About the lilting house and happy as the grass was green,
    The night above the dingle starry,
        Time let me hail and climb
    Golden in the heydays of his eyes,
And honoured among wagons I was prince of the apple towns
And once below a time I lordly had the trees and leaves
        Trail with daisies and barley
    Down the rivers of the windfall light.

This verse follows Wordsworth in the paradox of a child's being 'below' a time and yet also a lord. But the exuberance of the detailed description is made poignant by the poet acknowledging that all this life exists only under time's temporary permission. Like George Eliot's river, time has moved the poet away from his childhood, and however vivid the memory it is still only a memory and the real experience has passed.

▶ Compare Dylan Thomas' way of adopting the eye of childhood for his description of nature with that of William Golding in the extract from his novel *Free Fall* (Part 3, page 99).

The Romantics: the sublime and the gothic

In July 1797 some friends came to stay with Coleridge, but an accident confined him at home. While they were out on their walk he wrote 'This Lime-Tree Bower My Prison' in which he thinks of them passing through familiar and varied landscape, which he recreates by imagining their responses to it. They pause on a high point:

> So my Friend
> Struck with deep joy may stand, as I have stood,
> Silent with swimming sense; yea, gazing round
> On the wide landscape, gaze till all doth seem
> Less gross than bodily; and of such hues
> As veil the Almighty Spirit, when yet he makes
> Spirits perceive his presence.

'Swimming sense', 'seem' and 'veil' contribute to a blurring of the physical senses, which opens the way to new vision. Coleridge believed that it was imagination, rather than reason, which inspired such revelation; it unified lesser perceptions, however intense, into an intuitive understanding of the divine. Believing this, Coleridge made personal to himself the principles explored by Burke who distinguished the sublime from what is merely beautiful (see Part 1, page 33). In October 1797 Coleridge wrote to his friend John Thelwall:

> I can contemplate nothing but parts, and parts are all *little* – ! – My
> mind feels as if it ached to behold and know something *great*
> – something *one* and *indivisible* – and it is only in the faith of this
> that rocks or waterfalls, mountains or caverns give me the sense of
> sublimity or majesty!

The Italian artist Salvator Rosa (1615–1673) specialised in terrifying and turbulent landscapes; his pictures were well known and collected by northern Europeans on the Grand Tour. William Turner (1775–1851), often judged to be the greatest English artist, captured a sense of the sublime in his mingling of light and water in ways that dissolved boundaries. Like many of the Romantic poets, Turner was drawn to the mountains of Wales, the Lake District and the Swiss Alps. Like them, he sensed that light from above and water from below often combine to transfigure these high regions, generating a sense of human littleness beside the majesty of the natural world. Many of his works also convey unity of perception, Coleridge's wish for 'something one and indivisible'. Early in his career Turner was a skilled topographical draughtsman, but his later work depended on his impressions of landscape detail being indistinct. Gilpin wrote in 1791:

> Many images owe their sublimity to their *indistinctness*; and frequently what we call sublime is the effect of that heat and fermentation, which ensues in the imagination from its ineffectual efforts to conceive some dark, obtuse idea beyond its grasp. Bring the same within the compass of its comprehension, and it may continue *great*, but it will cease to be *sublime*.

Burke believed that a sense of the sublime lies less in the objective mountains, lakes and skies of nature and more in the subjective imagination that perceives or remembers them. A sense of the sublime is easier for the poet than the visual artist: whereas the one has to animate ideas with words, the other tries to represent them in paint. In Wordsworth's view, a poet is specially gifted in being 'endowed with more lively sensibility … and a more comprehensive soul than are supposed to be common among mankind'. He also believed that a child is more open than an adult to such overwhelming impressions. In his 'Ode: Intimations of Immortality' one of Wordsworth's most memorable images places small children alongside grandeur and infinity:

> And see the children sport upon the shore,
> And hear the mighty waters rolling evermore.

The sublime and the gothic often coincide; both characterise many of the Romantic poets and storytellers around 1800. Both explore beyond the confines of normal life, sometimes through physical journeys, but in general the gothic deals, often sensationally, with fear and horror, whereas the sublime evokes more exalted states of awe. Readers have found both in the fantastical tale of Coleridge's *The Ancient Mariner* (1798). His dream fragment 'Kubla Khan' (1798) reaches for the sublime, whereas 'Christabel' (1799), much praised in its day, seems to be more in the gothic tradition. The Brontë sisters set their celebrated novels *Wuthering Heights* (1846) and *Jane Eyre* (1847) in remote and forbidding places: Heathcliff's very name links the landscape with his nature. His literary origins may be found in dark monsters of the gothic tradition, but his mutual love with Catherine approaches the sublime and is fed by the landscape of their childhood. Both novels include intense feelings which can make normal morality and behaviour seem trivial.

Mary Shelley's *Frankenstein* (1818) is essentially a gothic tale, but the author evokes the sublime when Victor, despairing of what he has loosed into the world, makes a solitary expedition to the foothills of Mont Blanc:

> The abrupt sides of vast mountains were before me; the icy wall of the glacier overhung me; a few shattered pines were scattered around; and the solemn silence of this glorious presence-chamber of imperial nature was broken only by the brawling waves or the fall of some vast fragment, the thunder-sound of the avalanche or the cracking, reverberated along the mountains, of the accumulated ice, which, through the silent working of immutable laws, was ever and anon rent and torn, as if it had been but a plaything in their hands.

With narrative irony, this scene elevates Victor's spirits just before he sees the gothic horror of his created monster whose 'countenance bespoke bitter anguish, combined with disdain and malignity, while its unearthly ugliness rendered it almost too horrible for human eyes'.

▶ Compare Mary Shelley's scene in *Frankenstein* (the opening of Chapter 10) with Hopkins' description of a mountain (see page 71, below) and Shelley's *Mont Blanc* (Part 3, page 91). Consider especially the differences between precision and suggestiveness.

Hardy's Wessex

Thomas Hardy (1840–1928) set his novels in the south-western counties of Dorset and Wiltshire, reaching into parts of Hampshire, Somerset and Devon. When he wrote the magazine instalments of *Far from the Madding Crowd*, he adopted the old word 'Wessex' (in Anglo-Saxon England, the area of the West Saxons) because it gave him a large enough canvas for what became the rural environment for almost all his novels. He intended the word to denote 'a partly real, partly dream-country' in his books. But he misjudged the way his readers would seize on the name:

> ... and the dream-country has, by degrees, solidified into a utilitarian region which people can go to, take a house in, and write to the papers from. But I ask all good and idealistic readers to forget this, and to refuse steadfastly to believe that there are any inhabitants of a Victorian Wessex outside these volumes ...
>
> (from the author's preface to *Far from the Madding Crowd*, 1874)

Hardy is so meticulous in describing the landscape of his half-fictional Wessex that it is not surprising his readers were misled into thinking it actually existed. However, there is much in his landscape that is either unrealistic or strongly manipulated. For example, his rustic characters may live and act as authentic countrymen, but their speech (often as commentary on the main story) is far from that of real people. Hardy is also writing a personal elegy for a disappearing way of life; he takes a slightly detached, sometimes quizzical, stance so that even his scenery seems to wear a reflective dress of language in which the polysyllables often approach pedantry. In *The Return of the Native* (1878) he invents Egdon Heath. This landscape is not merely a background for the human action; it becomes a mysterious extra character with unpredictable moods:

> Throughout the blowing of these plaintive November winds that note bore a great resemblance to the ruins of human song which remain to the throat of fourscore and ten. It was a worn whisper, dry and papery, and it brushed so distinctly across the ear that, by the accustomed, the material minutiae in which it originated could be realised as by touch. It was the united products of infinitesimal vegetable causes, and these were neither stems, leaves, fruit, blades, prickles, lichen, nor moss.
>
> They were the mummied heath-bells of the past summer, originally tender and purple, now washed colourless by Michaelmas rains, and dried to dead skins by October suns. So low was an individual sound from these that a combination of hundreds only just emerged from silence, and the myriads of the whole declivity reached the woman's ear but as a shrivelled and intermittent recitative.

Hardy's poetry

Hardy was also a great poet, writing in various verse forms about relationships, the erratic workings of fate, personal memories, growing old – and almost always setting his poems within the natural world and country life around him. 'The Trampwoman's Tragedy' (pub. 1903) is written as a ballad, a traditional form that helps to give universal resonance to a particular incident. The ballad's repetitive rhythms match the daylong plodding of the four main characters:

> For months we had padded side by side,
> > Ay, side by side,
> Through the Great Forest, Blackmore wide,
> > And where the Parret ran.
> We faced the gusts on Mendip Ridge,
> Had crossed the Yeo unhelped by bridge,
> Been stung by every Marshwood midge,
> > I and my fancy man.

Whether or not the reader knows these forests, rivers and valleys, the very names are evocative and help to bring an old story close, as does the confiding and often wry manner of the speaker, the trampwoman who survives a great tragedy and is condemned to live tormented with memories.

Walking, more than riding or driving, takes time and brings the walker into close contact with both weather and landscape. It encourages productive leisure for reflection and detailed observation. From his earliest years, Hardy spent much of his travelling time on foot, as do the main characters in his novels: the opening scene of husband and wife in *The Mayor of Casterbridge* (1886); Tess going to see Angel Clare's family; Clym on Egdon Heath in *The Return of the Native* (1878).

'At Castle Boterel' (*Poems 1912–1913*) tells of an old man driving, not walking, through drizzling rain to a road junction. He recalls a love scene from his youth when he and a girlfriend talked as they climbed a hill. The poem seems to withhold as much as it explains: we know nothing of their conversation, of what the girl looked like, nor how the relationship ended. This reticence is teasingly enigmatic for those readers who expect Hardy to be rich in detail. Even the landscape description is sparse:

> Primaeval rocks form the road's steep border,
>   And much have they faced there first and last,
> Of the transitory in earth's long order;
>   But what they record in colour and cast
>   Is – that we two passed.

By keeping the rocks impassive and featureless, Hardy makes them allies of time, that challenges both human life and memory. Thus the forbidding landscape has symbolic value as well as being a place that can be accurately recorded.

Topology merges with history, as it does in his novel *The Mayor of Casterbridge* when Hardy describes the sinister Ring, a large Roman arena, just outside the town.

▶ Explore how Hardy uses landscape in his poems to support reflection or memory: 'The Darkling Thrush', 'The Voice', and 'Afterwards' are good starting points.

Women in Hardy's landscapes

Hardy realises that time moves on and brings no new security to match the lost idyll. He was writing against a background of the 19th-century's crisis of faith, Darwin's *The Origin of Species* (1859) and the alarming pace of industrialisation. This last is most vivid when Tess, the country girl, stands with the milk churns at the railway station and in a later scene feeds the threshing machine. She becomes a victim not just of modern material progress but also of old-fashioned moral prejudice. In between these ruthless extremes of future and past, Hardy gives her temporary escape, not just in a landscape setting but as part of nature itself:

> On these lonely hills and dales her quiescent glide was of a piece with
> the element she moved in. Her flexuous and stealthy figure became
> an integral part of the scene. At times her whimsical fancy would
> intensify natural processes around her till they seemed a part of her

own story. Rather they became a part of it; for the world is only a
psychological phenomenon, and what they seemed they were. The
midnight airs and gusts, moaning amongst the tightly-wrapped buds
and bark of the winter twigs, were formulae of bitter reproach.

Her total identification of spirit with the earth is intuitive, not intellectual. Tess
thinks herself inadequate, especially when, at Talbothays, she casts herself as
a disciple of the university-educated Angel Clare. But Hardy makes us (and,
eventually, Angel) value the purity of her intuitions; in this way, Tess, Hardy's
favourite heroine, can represent the vulnerability of the land.

In *Far from the Madding Crowd* his heroine Bathsheba also suffers, but,
unusually for his women, she is a landowner with status and powers of decision. At
a crisis in her marriage she withdraws from her farmhouse to spend a night in the
open air. The hollow she chooses as a refuge looks different in the morning light:

> But the general aspect of the swamp was malignant. From its moist
> and poisonous coat seemed to be exhaled the essences of evil things
> in the earth, and in the waters under the earth. The fungi grew in
> all manner of positions from rotting leaves and tree stumps, some
> exhibiting to her listless gaze their clammy tops, others their oozing
> gills. Some were marked with great splotches, red as arterial blood,
> others were saffron yellow, and others tall and attenuated, with
> stems like macaroni. Some were leathery and of richest browns.
> The hollow seemed a nursery of pestilences small and great, in the
> immediate neighbourhood of comfort and health …

▶ Contrast these two passages. How does the language convey a suffering state of
mind?

Observation and beyond

In his final section of 'Tintern Abbey' Wordsworth pays tribute to his sister Dorothy.
She was devoted to him throughout her life; she appreciated nature with similar
intensity and observed its detail more scrupulously. She was no poet but recorded
what she saw and felt in a journal 'because I shall give William pleasure by it'.

> When we were in the woods beyond Gowborrow Park we saw a few
> daffodils close to the water-side. We fancied that the lake had floated
> the seeds ashore, and that the little colony had so sprung up. But as
> we went along there were more and yet more; and at last, under the
> boughs of the trees, we saw that there was a long belt of them along
> the shore, about the breadth of a country turnpike road. I never saw
> daffodils so beautiful. They grew among the mossy stones about
> and about them; some rested their heads upon these stones as on a
> pillow for weariness; and the rest tossed and reeled and danced, and

seemed as if they verily laughed with the wind, that blew upon them over the lake; they looked so gay, ever glancing, ever changing.

(from Dorothy Wordsworth's *Journal*, Thursday April 15th, 1802)

Her brother used this description for his poem 'Daffodils'.

Gerard Manley Hopkins

The poet Gerard Manley Hopkins (1844–1889) also kept a journal. On July 20th 1868 he described the Rhone glacier.

It has three stages – first, a smoothly-moulded in a pan or theatre of thorny peaks, swells of ice rising through the snow-sheet and the snow itself tossing and fretting into the sides of the rock walls in spray-like points: this is the first stage of glaciers generally; it is like bright-plucked water swaying in a pail –; second, after a slope nearly covered with landslips of moraine, was a ruck of horned waves steep and narrow in the gut: now in the upper Grindelwald glacier between the bed or highest stage was a descending limb which was like the rude and knotty bossings of a strombous shell –; third, the foot, a broad limb opening out and reaching the plain, shaped like the fan-fin of a dolphin or a great bivalve shell turned on its face, the flutings in either case being suggested by the crevasses and the ribs by the risings between them, these being swerved and inscaped strictly to the motion of the mass.

'Inscape', for Hopkins, meant inner design or pattern. He concentrated hard to understand it in nature and to achieve it in his writing. He believed poetry to exist midway between prose and music, and much of the difficult obscurity for which he was criticised lies in his efforts to explore beyond the surface of what he saw in nature. Sometimes his verse seems knotted with compound words and strange word order, often elliptical with the absence of prepositions and other small functional words. He believed that the logic which is generally required in prose has only a minor role in poetry, where sounds, rhythms and word-associations are more vividly helpful in achieving inscape. Here are the two central verses of 'Inversnaid' (1881), a lively stream (or 'burn') in Scotland:

A windpuff bonnet of fawn-froth
Turns and twindles over the broth
Of a pool so pitchblack, fell-frowning,
It rounds and rounds despair to drowning.

Degged with dew, dappled with dew,
Are the groins of the braes that the brook treads through,
Wiry heathpacks, flitches of fern,
And the beadbonny ash that sits over the burn.

John Clare

Like Hopkins, John Clare (1793–1864) was interested in the minute workings and patterns of nature and both poets were driven to mental illness by the pressures of the world on their sensitive imaginations. In other ways they were very different. Hopkins was an Oxford intellectual and a Jesuit priest trying to relate to his parishioners in Liverpool and Dublin; Clare was a poor labourer who rarely travelled beyond his village of Helpston in Northamptonshire. But these limits were the source of his genius. His identity as a man and a poet was bound into his locality.

Clare's London publisher, John Taylor, kept faith with his 'peasant-poet', but often had to struggle with Clare's lack of interest in conventional grammar, punctuation, spelling and with his use of local dialect words. Clare's oddity sprang not from ignorance, but from his instinct that nature must not be subject to the structures that men often impose on their experiences. For example, in 'Emmonsails Heath in Winter' (between 1824 and 1832; quoted and analysed by John Barrell in *The Idea of Landscape and the Sense of Place*, 1972) Clare aims to express a continuum of connected impressions experienced simultaneously. But language is both ordered and sequential – hence the difficulty if an artist wants to record faithfully what he sees and feels in a form that is not visual:

> I love to see the old heaths withered brake
> Mingle its crimpled leaves with furze and ling   (*crimpled* crumpled)
> While the old heron from the lonely lake
> Starts slow and flaps his melancholy wing
> And oddling crow in idle motion swing   (*oddling* different
> On the half rotten ash trees topmost twig   from the other crows)
> Beside whose trunk the gipsey makes his bed
> Up flies the bouncing woodcock from the brig   (*brig* bridge)
> Where a bleak quagmire quakes beneath the tread
> The fieldfare chatter in the whistling thorn
> And for the awe round fields and closen rove   (*awe* haw; *closen* closes)
> And coy bumbarrells twenty in a drove   (*bumbarrels* long-tailed tits)
> Flit down the hedge rows in the frozen plain
> And hang on little twigs and start again.

The poem ends with the birds habitually starting again. Habit, as Wordsworth also believed, is more enriching than confining. 'Habit', with familiar and loving repetition, allows the poet also to 'inhabit' his small world, which is miniature but infinitely rich. Clare's recent biographer Jonathan Bate has noted his interest in roundness: molehills, small holes and, especially, birds' nests:

> A human being can do everything except build a bird's nest. What we can do is build an analogue of a bird's nest in a poem. We can make a verbal nest by gathering and cherishing odd scraps of language.

John Keats

On one level Keats' (1795–1821) much anthologised 'To Autumn' (1819) is a descriptive poem. 'To bend with apples the moss'd cottage trees', 'While barred clouds bloom the soft-dying day' – these are richly visual lines. However, the poet's observation feels part of a more organic response to the season and to time passing. He subsumes his 'I' (and his eye) into an address to the spirit of autumn, which, in the second verse, is personified into a woman; her spirit materialises in four different ways, all connected with the season's work, but all casual and drowsy. Both poet and reader become absorbed into autumn, helped by the subtlety of syntax: the first verse contains nothing as decisive as main verb. When one appears in line 12 it has the elusive quality of a question. The final verse refers to spring, but celebrates the compensations inherent in autumn – 'thou hast thy music too'. The poem slips from the visual to the aural, and the music of departing birds has a melancholy strain, as did Wordsworth's solitary reaper (see page 60, above). Both poets realise that music, as much as landscape, can minister to the imagination.

▶ Compare the descriptions of nature mentioned or quoted above (the two journals, 'Inversnaid', 'Daffodils', 'Emmonsails Heath in Winter', 'To Autumn') and those by Dorothy Wordsworth quoted in Part 3 (page 89). What differences do you find in the writers' approaches? Which for you is the most successful?

Working the land

Sometimes nature pours forth abundance, but it may be more honest to live a hard life in tough surroundings. Wordsworth's long narrative poem 'Michael', which appeared in *Lyrical Ballads* (1798), tells of a shepherd very unlike those in Renaissance pastorals. He is old, independent and hardworking. His house in a high Cumbrian valley is known as 'The Evening Star', as tribute to his age and the example he sets of virtuous living. Though faithful to his wife Isabel, he seems more at one with his surroundings, devoted to his duty and his sheep. Habit has brought him intuitive knowledge of the land, the weather and the health of his flock. The hills and fields

> ... had laid
> Strong hold on his affections, were to him
> A pleasurable feeling of blind love,
> The pleasure which there is in life itself.

Wordsworth gives no detailed features of the landscape, almost as if he needs to be as austere in his writing as Michael is in his life. The poem avoids anything decorative. He refers to 'winds', 'storm', 'streams and rocks', 'many thousand mists', so that the environment becomes part of Michael himself, rather than acting as simply background to his story.

Wordsworth follows on more from Virgil's *Georgics* than his *Eclogues* (see Part 1, page 12) in that it is Michael's work rather than leisure that creates harmony between man and the land. The American poet Richard Wilbur (born 1921) also celebrates work, but evokes a kinder landscape when he recalls a gardener who has died recently. Note how the poem's title flows into the first line, as though the humble simplicity of his life is part of the soil he tilled:

> *He was*
> a brown old man with a green thumb:
> I can remember the screak on stones of his hoe,
> The chug, choke, and high madrigal wheeze
> Of the spray-cart bumping below
> The sputtery leaves of the apple trees,
> But he was all but dumb
>
> Who filled some quarter of the day with sound
> All of my childhood long. For all I heard
> Of all his labours, I can now recall
> Never a single word
> Until he went in the dead of fall
> To the drowsy underground,
>
> Having planted a young orchard with so great care
> In that last year that none was lost, and May
> Aroused them all, the leaves saying the land's
> Praise for the livening clay,
> And the found voice of his buried hands
> Rose in the sparrowy air.

► How do sound and silence contribute to the optimism of Wilbur's elegy above?

Often readers of landscape poetry may be surprised that there is a voice in the land that takes you even closer to its heart than the poem's visual qualities. Keats' 'Ode to a Nightingale' and R.S. Thomas' 'A Blackbird Singing' work in this way. Many of Thomas' poems, such as 'Iago Prytherch' and 'A Gardener', are dark and gritty. For him working on the land has little to do with dwelling or empathy. 'A Muck Farmer' (pub. 1958), like Hardy's Tess at Flintcombe Ash, describes unrewarding drudgery:

> His rare smile,
> Cracked as the windows of his stone house
> Sagging under its weight of moss,
> Falls on us palely like the wan moon
> That cannot pierce the thin cloud
> Of March. His speech is a rank garden,
> Where thought is choked in the wild tangle
> Of vain phrases.

George Eliot

The scope of the novel, especially in the 19th century, invites readers to compare moral values amongst very different characters: intellectuals, prosperous aristocrats and landowners, doctors, clergymen – and ordinary men and women who live and work close to the land. George Eliot's *Middlemarch* (1872) offers a wide range of social types, including the Garth family. Caleb, a man of scrupulous integrity, is a land-manager, skilled in all practical matters. He, his wife and daughter appear unobtrusively in the novel, but soon become moral touchstones: we judge other characters according to how they judge the Garths.

In Chapter 56 Caleb is going to measure and value some land:

> It was one of those grey mornings after light rains, which become delicious about twelve o'clock, when the clouds part a little, and the scent of the earth is sweet along the lanes and by the hedgerows.

Leisurely appreciation suddenly stops as he encounters a dispute between some labourers and railway agents who are also measuring land. Caleb's involvement raises issues about 19th-century progress versus traditional ways of life; it becomes complicated when Fred Vincy passes by, an over-indulged but amiable young man who seems to have gained little from his university education. The next day, to the distress of Fred's snobbish parents, Caleb offers him a job; gradually he learns about hard work and how to manage land. His life now becomes more useful and thoroughly imbued with the virtues of the Garth family. George Eliot's approval and Fred's good fortune are confirmed when he marries Caleb's daughter Mary.

Eliot's earlier story of *Adam Bede* (1859) was very popular in its time. It is set wholly in a rural landscape that includes the Poysers' busy farm. Eliot invites moral judgements in favour of devoted work, social duty and self-sacrifice. Adam, the novel's young hero, has all these virtues, but also a sharply critical tongue that scourges all who fall short. Events bring him great suffering and he learns to curb this fault, so that by the end of the novel he has become a moral paragon, almost a Christ-figure. Critics who deplore Eliot's tendency to preach at her readers have noted that Adam is also a carpenter. Trees dominate landscapes; unlike stone, they are alive; they take time to mature; then their products serve man in peace and war. A carpenter's skill mediates between the trees' rough living state and their results in civilised life. A carpenter is close to nature and his profession may therefore stand for utility and honest dignity.

Only ten years earlier (1849) Millais, the **Pre-Raphaelite** artist, had exhibited *Christ in the House of his Parents*, now in the Tate Britain gallery. In the painting Joseph breaks off from his work on a wooden panel to help Mary comfort the child Jesus, who shows a wound in his palm. The window opens out to a pastoral landscape with sheep. The picture is full of major and minor symbolism (see Part 1, page 24). Christ started and ended his life with wood: he learned to be a carpenter; eventually he carried his wood and was crucified on it – so that a simple wooden cross became both the humblest and most triumphant symbol of all.

Desolated land

In 1962 the American biologist Rachel Carson published *Silent Spring*, which in the two years before her death sold nearly a million copies and soon became one of the most influential books of the century. It became a seminal text for the growing ecology movements and its power was evident from the savage and wayward attempts to discredit her work: one objector called her a 'hysterical woman'; another wondered 'why a spinster with no children was so interested in genetics'; another (a scientist who had much to lose if the book succeeded) thought that someone who wrote so well and with popular appeal couldn't be a serious scientist.

The book explains the effects of toxic chemicals on the countryside; Carson felt they should not be called 'insecticides', but 'biocides'. The sinister 'death-by-indirection' that they carry, she thought, is like Medea's poisoned robe for Jason's bride in Ovid's myth, or (in more modern analogies) like Grimm's fairy tales or the eerie cartoons of Charles Addams. The book begins almost as a fairy tale of her own:

> There was once a town in the heart of America where all life seemed to live in harmony with its surroundings. The town lay in the midst of a checkerboard of prosperous farms, with fields of grain and hillsides of orchards where, in spring, white clouds of bloom drifted above the green fields. In autumn, oak and maple and birch set up a blaze of colour that flamed and flickered across a backdrop of pines. The foxes barked in the hills and the deer silently crossed the fields, half-hidden in the mists of the autumn mornings.

Then a blight spreads through the land, the composite impact of all the poisons Carson will analyse in the chapters that follow:

> No witchcraft, no enemy action had silenced the rebirth of new life in this stricken world. The people had done it themselves.

In the book's title the spring is silent because 'no birds sing', a quotation she takes from Keats' strange poem 'La Belle Dame sans Merci' (1819), set like a medieval ballad in a desolated landscape. The poet questions a haggard knight, 'alone and palely loitering', who tells of meeting a lady and of being obsessed by her wild beauty. She takes him to her cave and lulls him to sleep. In his dream he sees 'pale kings and princes too', who lament and warn him that he is 'in thrall' – the word means bondage; from it comes 'enthral', much as 'captivate' relates to 'captive'.

Obsessive love has drained the knight of all energy and purpose, and the landscape, through pathetic fallacy, matches his deprivation:

> And that is why I sojourn here
>   Alone and palely loitering,
> Though the sedge has wither'd from the lake,
>   And no birds sing.

Though this last verse purports to explain why the story has happened and why he lingers by the desolate lake, the poem withholds more than it gives. Many critics see it as the expression of a weird psychological state: its core is a dream in a cave, enclosed by a journey, told by the knight to the poet, who tells it to us. The effect is of burrowing deep into the subconscious mind. Then the knight wakes and is suddenly propelled back into the landscape, where he is unable to re-orientate himself. All he can do, like Coleridge's Ancient Mariner, is to tell his tale to any poet who passes by. No doubt Rachel Carson, reading the last two lines – the first describing visual deprivation, the second aural – felt that a soundless landscape is more eerie than a disconcerting sight. Note how after the long penultimate line, the mere four syllables, 'And no birds sing', feel as though the poem has stopped rather than come to an end.

In Conrad's *Heart of Darkness* (1902), as with Keats' poem, the literal becomes psychological. But here the landscape of the riverbank is alien through being dense. A sense of loss is felt not through empty space, but through weird profusion. Marlow's journey up river is also a journey back in time and the penetration into a desolated soul:

> Going up that river was like travelling back to the earliest beginnings
> of the world, when vegetation rioted on the earth and the big trees
> were kings. An empty stream, a great silence, an impenetrable forest.
> The air was warm, thick, heavy, sluggish. There was no joy in the
> brilliance of sunshine … you thought yourself bewitched and cut off
> for ever from everything you had known once – somewhere – far
> away – in another existence perhaps.

'The people had done it themselves'

Unlike Keats, Rachel Carson puts responsibility for the blight firmly where it belongs: on human greed and negligence. So does Oliver Goldsmith in 'The Deserted Village' (1770). His poem is a protest against the effects of trade where all that matters is the profit-motive. The combination of enclosure (see Part 1, page 36), acquisitive landlords and the growth of industrial towns led to emigration from the land – and even from the country. In the village of Auburn, thought to be modelled on Goldsmith's childhood home in Ireland, the landscape and village community are traditionally interdependent. Like Carson, Goldsmith recognises that nature's balance is uniquely valuable, but fragile too and vulnerable to modern 'progress'.

Today also there are warnings about the threat to village communities. As it was in 1770, depopulation is a problem, but there is an additional threat now, that of introducing the wrong sort of prosperity through second homes for the wealthy, whose interest in the land is merely aesthetic and who cannot be part of an organic community.

Many readers will feel that the poem's value lies less in its description of the formerly contented village and more in the picture of current neglect – and in Goldsmith's moral philosophy, particularly his attack on the city's values of vanity and luxury. The mingled sounds of a once-thriving community have been reduced to single bird-cries, the lapwing and 'the hollow-sounding bittern', and a lonely old woman, 'yon widow'd, solitary thing', who begs for food and then weeps to herself through the night. Goldsmith describes her as the village's 'sad historian', because her memory and defeated, silent presence are more eloquent than the scholar's skill with language.

The desolation is made the more poignant because part of England has been lost: 'The cooling brook, the grassy-vested green' are gifts of a uniquely temperate climate. In its place, many of the dispossessed villagers are suffering in foreign landscapes:

> Those blazing suns that dart a downward ray,
> And fiercely shed intolerable day;
> Those matted woods where birds forget to sing,
> But silent bats in drowsy clusters cling;
> Those poisonous fields with rank luxuriance crown'd,
> Where the dark scorpion gathers death around …

In the four works mentioned above the landscape is made desolate by stillness more than by sound. This is also often the case in poems and prose that describe war. We think of war as being filled with horrifying noise, as it often is, but much writing about the Great War (1914–1918) suggests that the stillness of anticipation may be worse – or the silence after a barrage. In the extract in Part 3 (page 96) Edmund Blunden tells of entering the Schwaban Redoubt, where the intensity of the shells may be imagined by looking at the stillness of the aftermath. There are equally powerful passages in poems by Owen, Sassoon and Rosenberg, in Sebastian Faulks' *Birdsong* and Lyn Macdonald's collection of letters, *They Called it Passchendaele*.

Ancient and modern

Several modern poets have translated great works from the past. In doing so, their translations have become more personal reworkings, ways for each poet to adapt his or her poetic voice or, indeed, to find it extended through an earlier poet's inspiration. Recently the following have been published to great critical acclaim: Ted Hughes *Tales from Ovid* (1997); Seamus Heaney *Beowulf* (1999); Simon Armitage *Sir Gawain and the Green Knight* (2006).

It can be no coincidence that all three poets have robust styles ('visceral' is a common description) and the poems that have captured their attention are all powerful narratives, containing passion, pain and close human connection with nature and landscape.

Simon Armitage

Sir Gawain and the Green Knight (anon, *c.* 1400) clearly declares its origin in the seasonal rhythms of the year. In wintertime at King Arthur's court a young knight accepts a challenge from an imposing stranger (the Green Knight) to meet him in an unspecified place in the north in a year's time. The journey and the meeting will be a test of Gawain's courage. There will also be a test of his knightly discipline under sexual temptation. His mysterious opponent (also his generous host) has been interpreted in different symbolic ways, but his 'green' association with the earth gives him a special authority, which helps to validate the maturity that Gawain has gained when he returns to Arthur's court.

The medieval poet describes the passing of the year before Gawain begins his journey as a 'fast-forward' survey of the seasons, familiar to us as a modern technique in documentary television:

> Bot then hyyes harvest, and hardenes hym sone,
> Warnes hym for the winter to wax ful rype;
> He drives with droght the dust for to ryse,
> Fro the face of the folde to flyye ful hyghe;
> Wrothe wynde of the welkyn wrasteles with the sunne,
> The leves laucen fro the lynde and lighten on the grounde,
> And al grayes the gres that grene was ere;
> Thenne al rypes and rotes that ros upon first.
> And thus yirnes the yere in yisterdayes mony,
> And winter wyndes ayayn, as the worlde askes ...

Armitage's version of this appears as an extract in Part 3 (page 84), beginning with his line 'Then autumn arrives ...'.

▶ To appreciate this (in both versions), you need to recognise it as writing for oral delivery. Read both versions aloud, not too fast but conveying the poet's sense of unstoppable time. Listen to the vowel sounds and how they work with the forceful alliteration. Better still, both listen and read by alternating with a colleague. Does Armitage capture the aural qualities and the sense of an elemental landscape that appear in the original?

Ted Hughes

Ted Hughes (1930–1998) was an outsider who became Poet Laureate. Public responses to his work were complicated by his marriage to the American poet Sylvia Plath, their separation and her suicide. Some feminists and eco-critics have found him hypocritical in his view that the progress of the world has exiled mankind from nature, and brutally exploitative in seeming to celebrate male violence (see 'Feminist approaches, Part 4, page 105). He was born in a craggy part of Yorkshire, his family fished and hunted, and many of his poems (such as 'Pike' and the *Crow* sequence) describe nature's uncompromising brutality and celebrate the instinctive urge to survive. But he is capable of great tenderness: 'October Dawn' and 'Full Moon and Little Frieda' are delicate and atmospheric. Critics differ as to whether Hughes is better described as a nature poet, or as a poet who uses animals symbolically to acknowledge behaviour that has always been fundamental to created life. Many believe that his best work came last: *Tales from Ovid* was published a year before he died. The extract (Part 3, page 101) that ends the story of Myrrha links death and birth in a consummation with nature that is both painful and uplifting.

Seamus Heaney

As Ovid's stories provide the foundation for much western literature, the Old English epic *Beowulf* seems to speak for a northern culture that links heroic elegy with a strong sense of dark, austere landscapes. There is much in this poem to appeal to poets who inherit Celtic and Anglo-Saxon traditions. The poet Seamus Heaney used his own sense of belonging to the land and of growing up in a divided Ireland to respond to *Beowulf's* mixture of melancholy and primitive magic. Here is his version of the haunted mere, the lair of the monster Grendel who terrorises the local tribes:

> A few miles from here
> a frost-stiffened wood waits and keeps watch
> above a mere; the overhanging bank
> is a maze of tree-roots mirrored in its surface.
> At night there, something uncanny happens:
> the water burns. And the mere-bottom
> has never been sounded by the sons of men.
> On its bank, the heather-stepper halts:

the hart in flight from pursuing hounds
will turn to face them with firm-set horns
and die in the wood rather than dive
beneath its surface. That is no good place.
When wind blows up and stormy weather
makes clouds scud and the skies weep,
out of its depths a dirty surge
is pitched towards the heavens.

► How does Heaney's description of landscape contribute to a sense of fear? Compare it with the landscape of any gothic stories you know (see Part 1, page 34).

Heaney writes of finding a voice (often through someone else's words) before a poet finds his own voice, and before having something to say. The process is both mysterious and physical. Two of his early poems 'Digging' and 'The Diviner' establish the contrast; both are metaphors for finding the poem (rather than creating it), one through the metaphor of archaeology, the other through the inexplicable gift of the water-diviner. Commenting on 'Digging' (1964), Heaney spoke about 'poetry as a dig, a dig for finds that end up being plants'. 'The Diviner' is a play on words that links the man searching for water with the poet as mystic, a prophet engaged in divination. When read together, the poems describe men both engaged downwards with the earth and reaching up for new vision. By associating himself with men working on the land, Heaney suggests that poetry is also part of the land, as in one of his *Glanmore Sonnets*:

Vowels ploughed into other, opened ground,
Each verse returning like the plough turned round.   (Sonnet II)

In his early essay 'Feeling into Words' (1978) Heaney tells of being led into poetry by words as sound: he listened to language as different as Hopkins' poetry and the places listed in the radio shipping forecast. Responding to sound takes him to inchoate meanings, which then take him eventually towards poems. It can be no accident that when Heaney writes of the present, generally Ireland as it is now, it is often through digging into the past, into memories and traditions of the land.

A key to understanding Heaney's sense of the land and ancient memory can be found in 'The Sense of Place', from a lecture he gave in 1977. His examples are drawn largely from contemporary Ulster poets, but his and their roots lie in a Gaelic past. A merely visual pleasure or picturesque appreciation of landscape is shallow compared with 'our sense of ourselves as inhabitants not just of a geographical country but a country of the mind'. For Heaney the very names of places can resonate, so that their aural value is greater than what could be supplied by the eye alone.

One of Heaney's finest publications is *Field Work* (1979). Within it the sequence of *Glanmore Sonnets* describes the process of writing and simultaneously delivers its results:

> Vowels ploughed into other: opened ground.
> The mildest February for twenty years
> Is mist bands over furrows, a deep no sound
> Vulnerable to distant gargling tractors.
> Our road is steaming, the turned-up acres breathe.
> Now the good life could be to cross a field
> And art a paradigm of earth new from the lathe
> Of ploughs. My lea is deeply tilled.
> Old plough-socks gorge the subsoil of each sense
> And I am quickened with a redolence
> Of farmland as a dark unblown rose.
> Wait then ... Breasting the mist, in sowers' aprons,
> My ghosts come striding into their spring stations.
> The dream grain whirls like freakish Easter snows.   (Sonnet I)

▶ How does this poem about being a poet combine aural and visual effects into Heaney's awareness of the spirit of his landscape?

Thoreau, who evoked the spirit of the American wilderness (see Part 1, page 38) wrote in his essay 'Walking' (pub. 1862) that the poet was one who

> ... nailed words to their primitive sense, as farmers drive down stakes in spring, which the frost has heaved; who derived his words as often as he used them, – or transplanted them to his page with earth adhering to their roots, whose words were so true and fresh and natural that they would appear to expand like the buds at the approach of spring.

Assignments

1   Study any poem (or long extract) by Chaucer or Milton for their uses of landscape. Consider how they achieve visual effects as distinct from accurate and full versions of the landscape.

2   Read the extracts describing spring (Part 3, pages 86–87). Do you feel that their differences derive from the different times when the poets lived and from the literary conventions they were following?

3   Compare Keats' 'To Autumn' with the extract in Part 3 (page 88) describing the same time of year, from Thomson's 'The Seasons'.

4   Compare Hardy and any other 19th-century novelist or poet in their use of landscape as a context for love stories.

5   Given the inherent limitations of language, do you feel that accurate observation is either possible or sufficient for a writer to attempt? Do you value his or her work more if the writing takes you beyond observation? Here are some 20th-century poems to consider too: Edward Thomas ('The Brook', 'The Path'); Seamus Heaney ('Nesting Ground', 'Death of a Naturalist'); Ted Hughes ('The Horses'); Sylvia Plath ('Blackberrying').

3 | Texts and extracts

The texts and extracts that follow have been chosen to illustrate central themes and points made elsewhere in the book and to provide useful material for work on tasks and assignments.

Simon Armitage (translator)

From *Sir Gawain and the Green Knight* (anon, *c.* 1400)

The young knight Gawain has responded to a challenge made at King Arthur's court by a stranger, and his honour compels him to meet his opponent in a year's time – in other words, the next winter. The poet describes the passing of the year.

> but each year, short-lived, is unlike the last
> and rarely resolves in the style it arrived.
> So the festival finishes and a new year follows
> in eternal sequence, season by season.
> After lavish Christmas come the lean days of Lent
> when the flesh is tested with fish and simple food.
> Then the world's weather wages war on winter:
> cold shrinks earthwards and clouds climb;
> sun-warmed, shimmering rain comes showering
> onto meadows and fields where flowers unfurl,
> and woods and grounds wear a wardrobe of green.
> Birds burble with life and build busily
> as summer spreads, settling on slopes as
>   it should.
>   Now every hedgerow brims
>   with blossom and with bud,
>   and lively songbirds sing
>   from lovely, leafy woods.
>
> So summer comes in season with its subtle airs,
> when the west wind sighs among shoots and seeds,
> and those plants which flower and flourish are a pleasure
> as their leaves let drip their drink of dew
> and they sparkle and glitter when glanced by sunlight.
> Then autumn arrives to harden the harvest
> and with it comes a warning to ripen before winter.
> The drying airs arrive, driving up dust
> from the face of the earth to the heights of heaven,
> and wild sky wrestles the sun with its winds,
> and the leaves of the lime lay littered on the ground,

and grass that was green turns withered and grey.
Then all which had risen over-ripens and rots
and yesterday on yesterday the year dies away,
and winter returns, as is the way of the world
          through time.
      At Michaelmas the moon
      stands like that season's sign,
      a warning to Gawain
      to rouse himself and ride.

Geoffrey Chaucer

From *The Parlement of Foulys* (c. 1383)

The dreamer is led by his guide, Scipio Africanus, into the Garden of Love.

With that myn hand in his he tok anon,
Of whiche I confort caughte, and wente in faste.
But, Lord, so I was glad and wel begoon!
For overal where that I myne eyen caste
Were treis clad with leves that ay shal laste,
Eche in his kynde, of colour fresh and greene
As emeraude, that joye was to seene.

The byldere ok and ek the hardy asshe,
The piler elm, the cofre unto carayne;
The boxtre pipere, holm to whippis lashe;
The saylynge fyr; the cipresse deth to playne;
The shetere ew; the asp for shaftes pleyne;
The olyve of pes, and eke the dronke vyne;
The victor palm, the laurer to devyne.

A gardyn saw I, ful of blosmy bowes
Upon a ryver, in a grene mede,
There as swetnesse everemore inow is,
With floures white, blewe, yelwe and rede,
And colde welle-stremes, nothyng dede,
That swymmen ful of smale fishes lighte,
With fynnys rede and skales sylver-bryghte.

On every bow the bryddes herde I singe,
With voys of aungel in here armonye;
Some besyede hem here bryddes forth to brynge;
The litel conyes to here pley gone hye;
And ferther al aboute I gan aspye
The dredful ro, the buk, the hert and hynde,
Squyrels, and bestes smale of gentil kynde.

Thomas Carew

'The Spring' (1640)

Now that the Winter's gone, the earth hath lost
Her snow-white robes; and now no more the frost
Candies the grass, or casts an icy cream
Upon the silver lake or crystal stream:
But the warm sun thaws the benumbed earth,
And makes it tender; gives a sacred birth
To the dead swallow; wakes in hollow tree
The drowsy cuckoo and the humble-bee.
Now do a crowd of chirping minstrels bring
In triumph to the world the youthful Spring:
The valleys, hills, and woods in rich array
Welcome the coming of the long'd-for May.
Now all things smile: only my love doth lour,
Nor hath the scalding noonday sun the power
To melt that marble ice which still doth hold
Her heart congeal'd, and makes her pity cold.
The ox, which lately did for shelter fly
Into the stall, doth now securely lie
In open fields; and love no more is made
By the fireside, but in the cooler shade
Amyntas now doth with his Chloris sleep
Under a sycamore, and all things keep
      Time with the season: only she doth carry
      June in her eyes, in her heart January.

John Clare

From *The Shepherd's Calendar* (1827), from *May*

Each hedge is cover'd thick with green;
And where the hedger late hath been,
Young tender shoots begin to grow
From out the mossy stumps below.
But woodmen still on spring intrude,
And thin the shadow's solitude;
With sharpen'd axes felling down
The oak-trees budding into brown,
Which, as they crash upon the ground,
A crowd of labourers gather round.
These, mixing 'mong the shadows dark,

Rip off the crackling, staining bark,
Depriving yearly, when they come,
The green woodpecker of his home,
Who early in the spring began,
Far from the sight of troubling man,
To bore his round holes in each tree
In fancy's sweet security;
Now, startled by the woodman's noise,
He wakes from all his dreary joys.
The bluebells too, that thickly bloom
Where man was never known to come;
And stooping lilies of the valley,
That love with shades and dews to dally,
And bending droop on slender threads,
With broad hood-leaves above their heads,
Like white-robed maids, in summer hours,
Beneath umbrellas shunning showers;
These, from the bark-men's crushing treads,
Oft perish in their blooming beds.

Gerard Manley Hopkins

'Spring' (1877)

Nothing is so beautiful as spring –
  When weeds, in wheels, shoot long and lovely and lush;
  Thrush's eggs look little low heavens, and thrush
  Through the echoing timber does so rinse and wring
  The ear, it strikes like lightnings to hear him sing;
    The glassy peartree leaves and blooms, they brush
    The descending blue; that blue is all in a rush
  With richness; the racing lambs too have fair their fling.

What is all this juice and all this joy?
  A strain of the earth's sweet being in the beginning
In Eden garden. – Have, get, before it cloy,
  Before it cloud, Christ, lord, and sour with sinning,
Innocent mind and Mayday in girl and boy,
  Most, O maid's child, thy choice and worthy the winning.

John Milton

From *Paradise Lost* (1667), Book 4

Satan has made his entry into the Garden of Eden and he surveys its perfection.

> Thus was this place,
> A happy rural seat of various view;
> Groves whose rich Trees wept odorous Gumms and Balme,
> Others whose fruit burnish'd with Gold'n Rind
> Hung amiable, Hesperian Fables true,
> If true, here only, and of delicious taste:
> Betwixt them Lawns, or level Downs, and Flocks
> Grazing the tender herb, were interpos'd,
> Or palmy hillock, or the flow'ry lap
> Of some irriguous Valley spread her store,
> Flowers of all hue, and without Thorn the Rose:
> Another side, umbrageous Grots and Caves
> Of cool recess, o'er which the mantling Vine
> Lays forth her purple Grape, and gently creeps
> Luxuriant; meanwhile murmuring waters fall
> Down the slope hills, disperst, or in a Lake,
> That to the fringed Bank with Myrtle crown'd,
> Her crystal mirror holds, unite their streams.
> The birds their quire apply; airs, vernal airs,
> Breathing the smell of field and grove, attune
> The trembling leaves, while universal Pan
> Knit with the Graces and the Hours in dance
> Led on th'Eternal Spring. Not that fair field
> Of Enna, where Proserpine gath'ring flow'rs
> Her self a fairer flow'r by gloomy Dis
> Was gather'd, which cost Ceres all that pain
> To seek her through the World; nor that sweet Grove
> Of Daphne by Orontes, and th'inspir'd
> Castalian Spring, might with this Paradise
> Of Eden strive;

James Thomson

From *The Seasons* ('Autumn') (pub. 1730)

> Thus solitary, and in pensive Guise,
> Oft let me wander o'er the russet Mead,
> And thro' the sadden'd Grove, where scarce is heard
> One dying Strain, to cheer the Woodman's Toil.
> Haply some widow'd Songster pours his Plaint,

Far, in faint Warblings, thro' the tawny Copse.
While congregated Thrushes, Linnets, Larks,
And each wild Throat, whose artless Strains so late
Swell'd all the Music of the swarming Shades,
Robb'd of their tuneful Souls, now shivering sit
On the dead Tree, a dull-despondent Flock!
With not a Brightness waving o'er their Plumes,
And Nought save chattering Discord in their Note. ...
The pale descending year, yet pleasing still,
A gentler Mood inspires; for now the Leaf
Incessant rustles from the mournful Grove,
Oft startling such as, studious, walk below,
And slowly circles thro' the waving Air.
But should a quicker Breeze amid the Boughs
Sob, o'er the Sky the leafy Deluge streams;
Till choak'd, and matted with the dreary Shower,
The Forest-Walks, at every rising gale,
Roll wide the wither'd Waste, and whistle bleak.
Fled is the blasted Verdure of the Fields;
And, shrunk into their beds, the flowery Race
Their sunny Robes resign. Even what remain'd
Of bolder Fruits falls from the naked Tree;
And Woods, Fields, Gardens, Orchards, all around
The desolated Prospect thrills the Soul.

Dorothy Wordsworth

Extracts from her *Journals*

27th July 1800

After tea we rowed down to Loughrigg Fell, visited the white
foxglove, gathered wild strawberries, and walked up to view Rydale.
We lay a long time looking at the lake; the shores all embrowned
with the scorching sun. The ferns were turning yellow, that is, here
and there one was quite turned. We walked round by Benson's wood
home. The lake was now most still, and reflected the beautiful yellow
and blue and purple and grey colours of the sky. We heard a strange
sound in the Bainriggs wood, as we were floating on the water; it
seemed in the wood, but it must have been above it, for presently
we saw a raven very high above us. It called out, and the dome of
the sky seemed to echo the sound. It called again and again as it flew
onwards, and the mountains gave back the sound, seeming as if from
their centre; a musical bell-like answering to the bird's hoarse voice.
We heard both the call of the bird, and the echo, after we could see
him no longer.

On a tour of the continent, 11th August 1820
Our way continued through interchange of pastoral and forest ground. Crossed a bridge, and then had the stream to our left in a rocky gulf overhung with trees, chiefly beeches and elms; sawing-mills on the river very picturesque. It is impossible to imagine a more beautiful descent than was before us to the vale of Hasli. The roaring stream was our companion; sometimes we looked down upon it from the edge of a lofty precipice; sometimes descended towards it, and could trace its furious course for a considerable way. The torrent bounded over rocks, and still went foaming on, no pausing-places, no gentle windings, no pools under the innumerable smaller cataracts; the substance and the grey hue still the same, whether the stream rushed in one impetuous current down a regularly rough part of its steep channel, or laboured among rocks in cloud-shaped heavings, or in boisterous fermentation … We saw the cataract through an open window. It is a tremendous one, but, wanting the accompaniments of overhanging trees, and all the minor graces which surround our waterfalls – overgrowings of lichen, moss, fern, and flowers – it gives little of what may be called pleasure. It was astonishment and awe – an overwhelming sense of the powers of nature for the destruction of all things and of the helplessness of man – of the weakness of his will if prompted to make a momentary effort against such a force. What weight and speed of waters! And what a tossing of grey mist! Though at a considerable distance from the fall, when standing at the window, a shower of misty rain blew upon us.

Jane Austen

From *Sense and Sensibility* (1811), Chapter 18

Edward returned to them with fresh admiration of the surrounding country; in his walk to the village he had seen many parts of the valley to advantage; and the village itself, in a much higher situation than the cottage, afforded a general view of the whole which had exceedingly pleased him. This was a subject which ensured Marianne's attention, and she was beginning to describe her own admiration of these scenes, and to question him more minutely on the subjects that had particularly struck him, when Edward interrupted her by saying –

'You must not enquire too far, Marianne – remember, I have no knowledge in the picturesque, and I shall offend you by my ignorance and want of taste, if we come to particulars. I shall call hills steep which ought to be bold; surfaces strange and uncouth which ought to be irregular and rugged; and distant objects out of sight which ought only to be indistinct through the soft medium of a hazy atmosphere. You must be satisfied with such admiration as I can honestly give. I call it a very fine country – the hills are steep, the woods seem full of fine timber, and the valley looks comfortable and snug – with rich meadows and several neat farmhouses scattered here and there. It exactly answers my idea of a fine country, because it unites beauty with utility – and I dare say it is a picturesque one too because you admire it; I can easily believe it to be full of rocks and promontories, gray moss and brushwood, but these are all lost on me. I know nothing of the picturesque.'

'I am afraid it is but too true,' said Marianne; 'but why should you boast of it?'

'I suspect,' said Elinor, 'that to avoid one kind of affectation, Edward falls into another. Because he believes that many people pretend to more admiration of the beauties of nature than they really feel, and is disgusted with such pretensions, he affects greater indifference and less discrimination in viewing them himself than he possesses. He is fastidious, and will have an affectation of his own.'

'It is very true,' said Marianne, 'that admiration of landscape scenery is become a mere jargon. Everybody pretends to feel and tries to describe with the taste and elegance of him who first defined what picturesque beauty was. I detest jargon of every kind, and sometimes I have kept my feelings to myself, because I could find no language to describe them in but what was worn and hackneyed out of all sense and meaning.'

'I am convinced,' said Edward, 'that you really feel all the delight in a fine prospect which you profess to feel. But, in return, your sister must allow me to feel no more than I profess. I like a fine prospect, but not on picturesque principles. I do not like crooked, twisted, blasted trees. I admire them much more if they are tall, straight and flourishing. I do not like ruined, tattered cottages. I am not fond of nettles, or thistles, or heath blossoms. I have more pleasure in a snug farm-house than a watch-tower – and a troop of tidy, happy villagers please me better than the finest banditti in the world.'

Percy Bysshe Shelley

From 'Mont Blanc' (1816)

Some say that gleams of a remoter world
Visit the soul in sleep, – that death is slumber,
And that its shapes the busy thoughts outnumber
Of those who wake and live. – I look on high;
Has some unknown omnipotence unfurled

The veil of life and death? Or do I lie
In dream, and does the mightier world of sleep
Spread far around and inaccessibly
Its circles? For the very spirit fails,
Driven like a homeless cloud from steep to steep
That vanishes among the viewless gales!
Far, far above, piercing the infinite sky,
Mont Blanc appears, – still, snowy, and serene –
Its subject mountains their unearthly forms
Pile around it, ice and rock; broad vales between
Of frozen floods, unfathomable deeps,
Blue as the overhanging heaven, that spread
And wind among the accumulated steeps;
A desert peopled by the storms alone,
Save when the eagle brings some hunter's bone,
And the wolf tracks her there – how hideously
Its shapes are heaped around! Rude, bare, and high,
Ghastly, and scarred, and riven. – Is this the scene
Where the old Earthquake-daemon taught her young
Ruin? Were these their toys? Or did a sea
Of fire envelop once this silent snow?
None can reply – all seems eternal now.
The wilderness has a mysterious tongue
Which teaches awful doubt, or faith so mild,
So solemn, so serene, that man may be,
But for such faith, with nature reconciled;
Thou hast a voice, great Mountain, to repeal
Large codes of fraud and woe; not understood
By all, but which the wise, and great, and good
Interpret, or make felt, or deeply feel.

Matthew Arnold

From 'The Scholar-Gipsy' (1853)

The poet settles down in a secluded spot in the hills above Oxford to read an old book about an Oxford scholar who left his studies and his career ambitions. The scholar joined a company of vagabond gipsies and came to value their intuitive knowledge and powers of imagination above traditional book-learning.

For most, I know, thou lov'st retired ground.
    Thee, at the ferry, Oxford riders blithe,
        Returning home on summer nights, have met
    Crossing the stripling Thames at Bablock-hithe,
        Trailing in the cool stream thy fingers wet,

As the slow punt swings round;
And leaning backwards in a pensive dream,
And fostering in thy lap a heap of flowers
Pluck'd in shy fields and distant woodland bowers,
And thine eyes resting on the moonlit stream.

And then they land, and thou art seen no more.
Maidens who from the distant hamlets come
To dance around the Fyfield elm in May,
Oft through the darkening fields have seen thee roam,
Or cross a stile into the public way.
Oft thou hast given them store
Of flowers – the frail-leaf'd, white anemone –
Dark bluebells drench'd with dews of summer eaves –
And purple orchises with spotted leaves –
But none has words she can report of thee.

And, above Godstow Bridge, when hay-time's here
In June, and many a scythe in sunshine flames,
Men who through those wide fields of breezy grass
Where black-wing'd swallows haunt the glittering Thames,
To bathe in the abandon'd lasher pass,
Have often pass'd thee near
Sitting upon the river bank o'ergrown:
Mark'd thy outlandish garb, thy figure spare,
Thy dark vague eyes, and soft abstracted air;
But, when they came from bathing, thou wert gone.

At some lone homestead in the Cumnor hills,
Where at her open door the housewife darns,
Thou hast been seen, or hanging on a gate
To watch the threshers in the mossy barns,
Children, who early range these slopes and late
For cresses from the rills,
Have known thee watching, all an April day,
The springing pastures and the feeding kine;
And mark'd thee, when the stars come out and shine,
Through the long dewy grass move slow away.

George Eliot

From the opening of *The Mill on the Floss* (1860)

A wide plain, where the broadening Floss hurries on between its
green banks to the sea, and the loving tide, rushing to meet it, checks
its passage with an impetuous embrace. On this mighty tide the black

ships – laden with the fresh-scented fir-planks, with rounded sacks of oil-bearing seed, or with the dark glitter of coal – are borne along to the town of St Oggs, which shows its aged, fluted red roofs and the broad gables of its wharves between the low wooded hill and the river brink, tinging the water with a soft purple hue under the transient glance of this February sun. Far away on each hand stretch the rich pastures, and the patches of dark earth, made ready for the seed of broad-leaved green crops, or touched already with the tint of the tender-bladed autumn-sown corn. There is a remnant still of the last year's golden clusters of beehive ricks rising at intervals beyond the hedgerows; and everywhere the hedgerows are studded with trees: the distant ships seem to be lifting their masts and stretching their red-brown sails close among the branches of the spreading ash. Just by the red-roofed town the tributary Ripple flows with its lively current into the Floss. How lovely the little river is, with its dark, changing wavelets! It seems to me like a loving companion while I wander along the bank and listen to its low placid voice, as to the voice of one who is deaf and loving. I remember those large dipping willows. I remember the stone bridge.

John Steinbeck

From the opening of *The Grapes of Wrath* (1939)

To the red country and part of the grey country of Oklahoma the last rains came gently, and they did not cut the scarred earth. The ploughs crossed and recrossed the rivulet marks. The last rains lifted the corn quickly and scattered weed colonies and grass along the sides of the roads so that the grey country and the dark red country began to disappear under a green cover. In the last part of May the sky grew pale and the clouds that had hung in high puffs for so long in the spring were dissipated. The sun flared down on the growing corn day after day until a line of brown spread along the edge of each green bayonet. The clouds appeared, and went away, and in a while they did not try any more. The weeds grew darker green to protect themselves, and they did not spread any more. The surface of the earth crusted, a thin hard crust, and as the sky became pale, so the earth became pale, pink in the red country and white in the grey country.

In the water-cut gullies the earth dusted down in dry little streams. Gophers and ant lions started small avalanches. And as the sharp sun struck day after day, the leaves of the young corn became less stiff and erect; they bent in a curve at first, and then as the central ribs of strength grew weak, each leaf tilted downward. Then it was June, and the sun shone more fiercely. The brown lines on the corn

LANDSCAPE AND LITERATURE

leaves widened and moved in on the central ribs. The weeds frayed and edged back toward their roots. The air was thin and the sky more pale; and every day the earth paled.

In the roads where the teams moved, where the wheels milled the ground and the hooves of the horses beat the ground, the dirt crust broke and the dust formed. Every moving thing lifted the dust into the air; a walking man lifted a thin layer as high as his waist, and a wagon lifted the dust as high as the fence tops, and an automobile boiled a cloud behind it. The dust was long in settling back again.

D.H. Lawrence
From *The Rainbow* (1915), Chapter 1

So the Brangwens came and went without fear of necessity, working hard because of the life that was in them, not for want of the money. Neither were they thriftless. They were aware of the last halfpenny, and instinct made them not waste the peeling of their apple, for it would help to feed the cattle. But heaven and earth was teeming around them, and how should this cease? They felt the rush of the sap in spring, they knew the wave which cannot halt, but every year throws forward the seed to begetting, and, falling back, leaves the young-born on the earth. They knew the intercourse between heaven and earth, sunshine drawn into the breast and bowels, the rain sucked up in the day-time, nakedness that comes under the wind in autumn, showing the birds' nests no longer worth hiding. Their life and interrelations were such; feeling the pulse and body of the soil, that opened to their furrow for the grain, and became smooth and supple after their ploughing, and clung to their feet with a weight that pulled like desire, lying hard and unresponsive when the crops were to be shorn away. The young corn waved and was silken, and the lustre slid along the limbs of the men who saw it. They took the udder of the cows, the cows yielded milk and pulse against the hands of the men, the pulse of the blood of the teats of the cows beat into the pulse of the hands of the men. They mounted their horses, and held life between the grip of their knees, they harnessed their horses at the wagon, and, with hand on the bridle-rings, drew the heaving of the horses after their will.

In autumn the partridges whirred up, birds in flocks blew like spray across the fallow, rooks appeared on the grey, watery heavens, and flew cawing into the winter. Then the men sat by the fire in the house where the women moved about with surety, and the limbs and the body of the men were impregnated with the day, cattle and earth and vegetation and the sky, the men sat by the fire and their brains were inert, as their blood flowed heavy with the accumulation from the living day.

The women were different. On them too was the drowse of blood-intimacy, calves sucking and hens running together in droves, and young geese palpitating in the hand while the food was pushed down their throttle. But the women looked out from the blind, heated intercourse of farm-life to the spoken world beyond. They were aware of the lips and the mind of the world speaking and giving utterance, they heard the sound in the distance, and they strained to listen.

Edmund Blunden

From *Undertones of War* (1928)

It was now approaching the beginning of November, and the days were melancholy and the colour of clay. We took over that deathtrap known as the Schwaben Redoubt, the way to which led through the fallen fortress of Thiepval. One had heard the worst accounts of the place, and they were true. Crossing the Ancre again at Black Horse Bridge, one went up through the scanty skeleton houses of Authuille, and climbing the dirty little road over the steep bank, one immediately entered the land of despair. Bodies, bodies and their useless gear heaped the gross waste ground; the slimy road was soon only a mud track which passed a whitish tumulus of ruin with lurking entrances, some spikes that had been pine trees, a bricked cellar or two, and died out. The village pond, so blue on the map, had completely disappeared. The Ligne de Pommiers had been grubbed up. The shell-holes were mostly small lakes of what was no doubt merely rusty water, but had a red and foul semblance of blood. Paths glistened weakly from tenable point to point. Of the dead, one was conspicuous. He was a Scottish soldier, and was kneeling, facing east, so that one could scarcely credit death in him; he was seen at some little distance from the usual tracks, and no-one had much time in Thiepval just then for sight-seeing, or burying. Death could not kneel so, I thought, and approaching I ascertained with a sudden shrivelling of spirit that Death could and did.

Beyond the area called Thiepval on the map a trench called St Martin's Lane led forward; unhappy he who got into it! It was blasted out by intense bombardment into a broad shapeless gorge, and pools of mortar-like mud filled most of it. A few duckboards lay half-submerged along the parapet, and these were perforce used by our companies, and calculatingly and fiercely shelled at moments by the enemy. The wooden track ended, and then the men fought their way on through the gluey morass, until not one or two were reduced to tears and impotent wild cries to God. They were not yet at the worst of their duty, for the Schwaben Redoubt ahead was an almost obliterated cocoon of trenches in which mud, and death, and life were much the same thing – and there the deep dugouts, which faced the German guns, were cancerous with torn bodies, and to pass an entrance was to gulp poison; in one place a corpse had apparently been thrust in to stop up a doorway's dangerous displacement, and an arm swung stupidly. Men of the next battalion were found in mud up to the armpits, and their fate was not spoken of; those who found them could not get them out. The whole zone was a corpse, and the mud itself mortified.

Stella Gibbons

From *Cold Comfort Farm* (1932), Chapter 3

Dawn crept over the Downs like a sinister white animal, followed by the snarling cries of a wind eating its way between the black boughs of the thorns. The wind was the furious voice of this sluggish animal light that was baring the dormers and mullions and scullions of Cold Comfort Farm.

The farm was crouched on a bleak hillside, whence its fields, fanged with flints, dropped steeply to the village of Howling a mile away. Its stables and outhouses were built in the shape of a rough octangle surrounding the farmhouse itself, which was built in the shape of a rough triangle. The left point of the triangle abutted on the farthest point of the octangle, which was formed by the cowsheds, which lay parallel with the big barn. The outhouses were built of rough-cast stone, with thatched roofs, while the farm itself was built partly of local flint, set in cement, and partly of some stone brought at great trouble and enormous personal expense from Perthshire.

The farmhouse was a long, low building, two-storied in parts. Other parts of it were three-storied. Edward the Sixth had originally owned it in the form of a shed in which he housed his swineherds, but he had grown tired of it, and had had it rebuilt in Sussex clay. Then he pulled it down. Elizabeth had rebuilt it, with a good many chimneys in one way and another. The Charleses had let it alone; but William and Mary had pulled it down again, and George the First had rebuilt it. George the Second, however, burned it down. George the Third added another wing. George the Fourth pulled it down again.

By the time England began to develop that magnificent blossoming of trade and imperial expansion which fell to her lot under Victoria, there was not much of the original building left, save the tradition that it had always been there. It crouched, like a beast about to spring, under the bulk of Mockuncle Hill. Like ghosts embedded in brick and stone, the architectural variations of each period through which it had passed were mute history. It was known locally as 'The King's Whim'.

…The front door of the farm faced a perfectly inaccessible ploughed field at the back of the house; it had been the whim of Red Raleigh Starkadder, in 1835, to have it so; and so the family always used to come in by the back door, which abutted on the general yard facing the cowsheds. A long corridor ran half-way through the house on the second storey and then stopped. One could not get into the attics at all. It was all very awkward.

… Growing with the viscous light that was invading the sky, there came the solemn tortured-snake voice of the sea, two miles away, falling in sharp folds upon the mirror-expanses of the beach.

Under the ominous bowl of the sky a man was ploughing the sloping field immediately below the farm, where the flints shone bone-sharp and white in the growing light. The ice-cascade of the wind leaped over him, as he guided the plough over the flinty runnels. Now and again he called roughly to his team:

'Upidee, Travail! Ho, there, Arsenic! Jug-jug!' But for the most part he worked in silence, and silent were his team. The light showed no more of his face than a grey expanse of flesh, expressionless as the land he ploughed, from which looked out two sluggish eyes.

T.S. Eliot

From *Little Gidding*, the last of *Four Quartets* (1935–1942)

Midwinter spring is its own season
Sempiternal though sodden towards sundown,
Suspended in time, between pole and tropic.
When the short day is brightest, with frost and fire,
The brief sun flames the ice, on pond and ditches,
In windless cold that is the heart's heat,
Reflecting in a watery mirror
A glare that is blindness in the early afternoon.
And glow more intense than blaze of branch, or brazier,
Stirs the dumb spirit: no wind, but pentecostal fire
In the dark time of the year. Between melting and freezing
The soul's sap quivers. There is no earth smell
Or smell of living thing. This is the spring time
But not in time's covenant. Now the hedgerow

Is blanched for an hour with transitory blossom
Of snow, a bloom more sudden
Than that of summer, neither budding nor fading,
Not in the scheme of generation.
Where is the summer, the unimaginable
Zero summer?

         If you came this way,
Taking the route you would be likely to take
From the place you would be likely to come from,
If you came this way in may time, you would find the hedges
White again, in May, with voluptuary sweetness.
It would be the same at the end of the journey,
If you came at night like a broken king,
If you came by day not knowing what you came for,
It would be the same, when you leave the rough road
And turn behind the pig-sty to the dull façade
And the tombstone. And what you thought you came for
Is only a shell, a husk of meaning
From which the purpose breaks only when it is fulfilled
If at all. Either you had no purpose
Or the purpose is beyond the end you figured
And is altered in fulfilment. There are other places
Which also are the world's end, some at the sea jaws,
Or over a dark lake, in a desert or a city –
But this is the nearest, in place and time,
Now and in England.

William Golding

From *Free Fall* (1959)

Two children trespass into a general's grounds. This is a daring adventure because there is a policeman outside to arrest them and they imagine lions inside waiting to savage them. The adrenalin of excitement turns a real garden into a vision.

> Slowly the noises of people died down and our tremors died away
> with them so that the lions were forgotten. The high parapet of the
> house began to shine, a full moon lugged herself over the top and
> immediately the gardens were translated. There was a silver wink
> from a pool nearer the house, cypresses, tall and hugely still, turned
> one frosted side to her light. I looked at Johnny and his face was
> visible and bland. Nothing could hurt us or would hurt us. We stood
> up and began to wander without saying anything. Sometimes we
> were waist-deep in darkness and then again drowned and then out in
> full light. Statues meditated against black deepnesses of evergreen

and corners of the garden were swept by dashes of flowering trees that at that month were flowering nowhere else. There was a walk with stone railings on our right and a succession of stone jars with stone flowers draped round them. This was better than the park because forbidden and dangerous; better than the park because of the moon and silence; better because of the magic house, the lighted windows and the figure pacing by them. This was a sort of home …

What was the secret of the strange peace and security we felt? Now if I invent I can see us from outside, starry-eyed ragamuffins, I with nothing but shirt and trousers, Johnny with not much more, wandering together through the gardens of the great house. But I never saw us from outside. To me, then, we remain these two points of perception, wandering in paradise. I can only guess our innocence, not experience it. If I feel a kindly goodwill towards the ragamuffins, it is towards two unknown people. We went slowly towards the trees where the wall had broken down. I think we had a kind of faith that the policeman would be gone and that nothing would embarrass us. Once, we came to a white path and found too late that it was new, unset concrete where we slid; but we broke nothing else in the whole garden – we took nothing, almost we touched nothing. We were eyes.

Before we buried ourselves in undergrowth again, I turned to look back. I can remember this. We were in the upper part of the garden, looking back and down. The moon was flowering. She had a kind of sanctuary of light around her, sapphire. All the garden was black and white. There was one tree between me and the lawns, the stillest tree that ever grew, a tree that grew when no-one was looking. The trunk was huge and each branch splayed up to a given level; and there, the black leaves floated out like a level of oil on water. Level after horizontal level these leaves cut across the splaying branches and there was a crumpled, silver-paper depth, an ivory quiet beyond them. Later, I should have called the tree a cedar and passed on, but then, it was an apocalypse.

Angela Carter

From 'The Erl-King' in *The Bloody Chamber and Other Stories* (1979)

The lucidity, the clarity of the light that afternoon was sufficient to itself; perfect transparency must be impenetrable, these vertical bars of a brass-coloured distillation of light coming down from sulphur-yellow interstices in a sky hunkered with grey clouds that bulge with more rain. It struck the wood with nicotine-stained fingers, the leaves glittered. A cold day of late October, when the withered blackberries dangled like their own dour spooks on the discoloured brambles. There were crisp husks of beechmast and cast acorn cups underfoot in the russet slime of dead bracken where the rains of the equinox had so soaked the earth that the cold oozed up through the soles of the shoes, lancinating cold of the approaching of winter that grips hold of your belly and squeezes it tight. Now the stark elders have an anorexic look; there is not much in the autumn wood to make you smile but it is not yet, not quite yet, the saddest time of the year. Only, there is a haunting sense of the imminent cessation of being; the year, in turning, turns in on itself. Introspective weather, a sickroom hush.

The woods enclose. You step between the fir trees and then you are no longer in the open air; the wood swallows you up. There is no way through the wood any more, this wood has reverted to its original privacy. Once you are inside it, you must stay there until it lets you out again for there is no clue to guide you through in perfect safety; grass grew over the track years ago and now the rabbits and foxes make their own runs in the subtle labyrinth and nobody comes. The trees stir with a noise like taffeta skirts of women who have lost themselves in woods and hunt round hopelessly for the way out. Tumbling crows play tig in the branches of the elms they clotted with their nests, now and then raucously cawing. A little stream with soft margins of marsh runs through the wood but it has grown sullen with the time of the year; the silent, blackish water thickens, now, to ice. All will fall still, all lapse.

A young girl would go into the wood as trustingly as Red Riding Hood to her granny's house but this light admits no ambiguities and, here, she will be trapped in her own illusion because everything in the wood is exactly as it seems.

Ted Hughes

From *Tales from Ovid* (1997)

This passage concludes the story of Myrrha, whose incestuous passion for her father led to the birth of Adonis. Near the end of her pregnancy, she asks the gods to prevent her from contaminating the world if she lives and the dead if she dies. She begs for some third way.

A power in the air hears the last prayer
Of the desperate. Myrrha's prayer to be no part
Of either her life or her death was heard and was answered.

The earth gripped both her ankles as she prayed.
Roots forced from beneath her toenails, they burrowed
Among deep stones to the bedrock. She swayed,

Living statuary on a tree's foundations.
In that moment, her bones became grained wood,
Their marrow pith,

Her blood sap, her arms boughs, her fingers twigs,
Her skin rough bark. And already
The gnarling crust has coffined her swollen womb.

It swarms over her breasts. It warps upwards
Reaching for her eyes as she bows
Eagerly into it, hurrying the burial

Of her face and her hair under thick-webbed bark.
Now all her feeling has gone into wood, with her body.
Yet she weeps,

The warm drops ooze from her rind.
These tears are still treasured.
To this day they are known by her name – Myrrh.

Meanwhile the meaty fruit her father implanted
Has ripened in the bole. Past its term,
It heaves to rive a way out of its mother.

But Myrrha's cramps are clamped in the heart-wood's vice.
Her gagged convulsions cannot leak a murmur.
She cannot cry to heaven for Lucina.

Nevertheless a mother's agony
Strained in the creaking tree and her tears drench it.
For pity, heaven's midwife, Lucina,

Lays her hands on the boughs in their torment
As she recites the necessary magic.
The trunk erupts, the bark splits, and there tumbles

Out into the world with a shattering yell
The baby Adonis.

Critical approaches

- How may modern theories of land and landscape affect our reading of texts from different periods?

- Are we justified in responding to landscape in literature merely in aesthetic terms?

Political approaches

Political interpreters of landscape writing deplore the vacuum in which it is sometimes read. Most land is owned by someone, people live and work on it, or visit it as tourists. Therefore there is bound to be a political context:

- How did it come to be owned?

- Who works on it and what are their conditions of work?

- What is the relationship of owner, workers and visitors?

- What is the agenda (acknowledged or not) of the poet or novelist when they describe the land?

A traditional critic may accept social hierarchy in which, for example, noblemen, tenant farmers and peasants all have their rightful places. An idealist may believe that there is a clear distinction between the false, materialistic city and the integrity of nature, without paying much attention to pastoral as a literary invention.

However, since about 1970 some political theorists have begun to question the assumptions behind pastoral and similar genres. The traditional pastoral idyll, suggesting that happy peasants live self-sufficient lives, is a fiction masking the truth that town and country depend on each other: in real life farmers need to sell their meat and wool in the town; they are vulnerable to bad weather, war and plague. When they survive, it is through hard work and shrewd commercial sense.

A materialist view will point out that there has never been an idyllic community in which all are equal. Nostalgia has invented a Golden Age where there was time for happy peasants to enjoy leisure and that somehow the land got cultivated and gave them the money on which to live. In reality, the medieval feudal system gave virtually no rights to the peasantry; later, when wealth depended more on trade, the profit motive continued to suppress those who worked on the land. Capitalism, generally thought to appear in the new cities with the Industrial Revolution in the late 18th century, can be traced far back to the city-states of the Italian Renaissance and was firmly rooted as agrarian capitalism in England from the 16th century.

Most of the great country houses, which tourists now visit with camera and guidebook as the essence of honest Old England, were built from exploiting the land and the impoverished classes that lived there. Poets who celebrated houses such as Penshurst and Saxham (see Part 2, page 56) probably had a vested interest in flattering the nobleman and in boosting his public image. It is an aristocratic myth that social inequalities were divinely ordained. Modern views of democracy are very different from those in the mid-19th century that happily assumed that the poor man was happy to be poor!

A Marxist critic will urge that we should read landscape literature with attention to social truths as well as to poetic artifice. Even Goldsmith in 'The Deserted Village' (see Part 2, page 77) decorates 'Sweet Auburn' with a nostalgic wash, which is literary rather than real, in order to highlight the poem's real point: the ruthless effects of agrarian capitalism on tenants and labourers which have reduced the village to its current plight. In 'The Village' (1783) Crabbe associates poets with the process of exploitation:

> I grant indeed that fields and flocks have charms
> For him that grazes or for him that farms;
> But when amid such pleasing scenes I trace
> The poor laborious natives of the place,
> And see the mid-day sun, with fervid ray,
> On their bare heads and dewy temples play;
> While some, with feebler heads and fainter hearts,
> Deplore their fortune, yet sustain their parts;
> Then shall I dare these real ills to hide
> In tinsel trappings of poetic pride?

▶ What are Crabbe's methods here of conveying his point of view?

Most landscape description aims to provide context for human life, but it is evident how rarely people are individualised unless they are members of the ruling classes. Note, for example how much 18th-century landscape painting shows the wealthy family, beautifully dressed, relaxing on a raised patch of ground and looking out across their productive land. Typically, the landowner will be alongside his young heir, and his wife surrounded by the younger children, perhaps under a tree that supplies shade and symbolically suggests (as a 'family' tree) that she is as fertile as the land. If any of their labourers are included, they will be small in the distance, their faces blurred or averted, making them part of the general landscape.

Even the artist John Constable, working and famous throughout the Romantic period for his scenes of ordinary life, rarely makes his workers seem individual. It was Wordsworth who notably broke with this tradition: see his poems 'The Pedlar', 'The Cumberland Beggar' and several of the shorter *Lyrical Ballads*, which put 'humble life' at the centre of his work. But even he rarely visualises the people or even gives them real character; instead, they have an intuitive or spiritual dimension, so that they can transmit Wordsworth's philosophy on how people and nature interact.

The critic Raymond Williams in *The Country and the City* (1973) objects to the patronising treatment of labourers. Reacting to 'Lob' by the **Georgian** poet Edward Thomas, he deplores

> a version of history which succeeds in cancelling history. All countrymen, of all conditions and periods, are merged into a single legendary figure … a working man becoming 'my ancient' and then the casual figure of a dream of England … The self-regarding patriotism of the high English imperialist period found this sweetest and most insidious of its forms in a version of the rural past.

The editors of the anthology *English Pastoral Verse* (1984) share Williams' bracing demands that poets tell the truth about rural life. However, since then other critics have reacted against these strictures. Jonathan Bate in *Romantic Ecology* (1994) finds limits in a strictly political approach; Seamus Heaney, reviewing the anthology, and especially its editorial angle, criticises 'a certain attenuation of response, so that consideration of the selected poems as made things, as self-delighting buds on the old bough of a tradition, is much curtailed'. As a poet he values 'the satisfaction of aural and formal play out of which poems arise'.

Feminist approaches

Plato, speculating on cosmology in the *Timaeus*, saw the soul of the whole world as female and the earth as our nurse. **Neo-platonic** thinkers in the Middle Ages linked this with Christian belief: the goddess Nature is subordinate to God and acts as midwife to turn abstract ideas into material life. Nature was often presented visually, wearing a robe decorated with creatures from water and land, plants and trees – and with flowers on her shoes. Dame Nature ('vicayre of the almighty lord') presides in Chaucer's 'Parlement of Foulys', holding on her wrist the most perfect female eagle; beneath her is the hierarchy of creation, each in its correct place and subject to Nature's judgement.

Modern ecology movements aim to restore a greater respect for 'mother' nature, which has been damaged by male greed and aggression. Science and technology have asserted man's mastery and plundered the earth's resources; men have treated nature as a passive, acquiescent female who must constantly supply them with comfort and nourishment. In traditional cultures, it was common for miners, burrowing as in a womb for minerals, to perform ceremonies of propitiation to the deities of the soil and as an apology to the mother.

Carolyn Merchant, in *The Death of Nature* (1980), writes that:

> The female earth was central to the organic cosmology that was undermined by the Scientific Revolution and the rise of a market-oriented culture in early modern Europe.

'Organic' is an important principle. So is interdependence. In medieval Europe small communities, largely agricultural, observed the cycles of nature and depended on habit, tradition and rituals, often linked with fertility cults. They believed that everything created was interconnected, and so they could speak of the earth as being like a human body and of the 'body' politic as a way of describing large and complex social groups.

The female principle of natural change (recurring birth, life and death) is fixed within the predictable stability of good order and supported by a sense of hierarchy within nature. But unpredictable change is alarming when nature produces storms, earthquakes and plagues. This destructive force was also seen as an aspect of the female – hence men's savage treatment of (female) witches, who attack established hierarchy, especially through contact with spirits. Witches' use of 'familiars' is a random type of animism, very different from the coherent spiritual force of neo-platonism.

Thus, in medieval life and literature, women may be variously goddesses, icons of courtly love, fertile mothers, pure virgins or witches to be hunted down. Sexual desire could be an enriching and civilising power, necessary for reproduction, but also a trap to enslave and destroy men.

When writing *Howards End* (1910) E.M. Forster was well aware of male assertiveness and female intuition. The male Wilcoxes are brusque, commanding, they work in the city and know all about money, progress and motor cars: 'telegrams and anger' is Forster's succinct and suggestive summary of their world. However, Margaret and the Schlegels are literary, intellectual and believe in the emotional life. Mrs Wilcox represents a different type of female principle: she has little knowledge and no opinions, but she and the spirit of the house are as one; she intends that the house pass after her death not to her materialistic children but to Margaret. The house and its meadows, deep in the heart of England, are essentially female, and the final scene of the novel shows women and children occupying the place. The Wilcoxes have lost their rights and Forster intends to show that a deeper (and female) principle of the land has survived and won.

Ecological approaches

The word *ecology* was coined in 1879 and derives from the Greek *oikos*, meaning a habitation or dwelling, and *logia*, an expression or study. Ecology is essentially an area of scientific study, but it has an obvious and lively political dimension which is growing rapidly in the 21st century. There is also cross-fertilisation between ecology and the more traditional disciplines of ethics, philosophy, art history, psychology and literature.

Much literary eco-criticism pays attention to pastoral and Romantic writing which values wild places, deplores many effects of industrialisation, and celebrates the vulnerable beauties of nature. In his *Romantic Ecology* (1991) Jonathan Bate draws attention to the inter-disciplinary nature of eco-criticism:

> History has dominated much recent discussion of literature, but geography also has its claims; we live and die as part of the body politic, but we also live and die in a place.

Ways of living and dying have always provided the subject matter of literature; Bate is indicating the range of contexts in which our living and dying takes place.

English pastoral, especially when playful and artificial, is essentially aesthetic. American pastoral is often agrarian, based on land-owning farmers contributing to a prosperous democracy, where the nostalgia evokes, not a classical idyll or Garden of Eden, but the 17th-century republican ideals of America's founding fathers. A different strand derives from Thoreau's *Walden* (see Part 1, page 38) and celebrates the wilderness, often coloured by masculine ideals of self-sufficiency on a western frontier. This sense of adventure is inherent in the comparatively recent history of a young country – but so too is the value of home.

Eco-critics value human rootedness, of dwelling in a home, as distinct from living in a house. In *Paradise Lost* (see Part 2, page 52) Milton idealises the bower that nature contrives for Adam and Eve to dwell; the values that underlie the description would be very familiar to members of today's activist Green parties. 'Dwelling' in full identification with the earth is more likely to be achieved in a rural culture than in cities. Cities promote a mobile culture in which our energy and ambition are praised if we are restless and rarely satisfied. Much of today's television urges us to keep changing our work, appearance, lifestyle, and the place where we live; celebrity culture often seems to applaud even those who change their partners.

John Clare (see Part 2, page 72) most clearly embodies the values of eco-critics because he resists change, except for the recurring and organic processes of birth, growth, death and renewal. In 1832 he wrote 'The Flitting' (departure) when forced to leave his home in Helpston where he had grown up. He moved to Northborough, only three miles away, but the significance of the disruption meant more to him than the distance:

> I miss the heath, its yellow furze
> Molehills and rabbit tracks that lead
> Through beesom ling and teasel burrs
> That spread a wilderness indeed
> The woodland oaks and all below
> That their white powdered branches shield
> The mossy pads – the very crow
> Croaked music in my native fields ...

Whereas Clare departs, Edward Thomas (1878–1917) returns in his poem 'Home', but with similar values of dwelling and memory. He describes his approach to the place he knows:

> One nationality
> We had, I and the birds that sang,
> One memory.

'Nationality' feels alien in the poem's simple diction, but the impact of its awkwardness is to reverse our easily assumed expectations. We are often encouraged to feel at home in our own nation, whereas 'home' for the eco-poet is a deeper ideal: to dwell in a remembered place rather than to live in a country for which we can feel patriotic. Thomas' split identity as an Anglo-Welsh poet may have made him especially aware of how individual identity can be as fragile as an eco-system.

A danger of extreme eco-criticism is that it may judge a poem or novel exclusively according to its green agenda. Shallow ecology emphasises human duty as steward of nature; a deep ecologist sees man simply as a part of a greater eco-system. For example, though some may praise Wordsworth for rejecting cities and finding his soul in landscape, his brand of nature depends on what it offers to humankind, not in economic terms, but in spiritual communion. A deep eco-critic would relegate human needs (even Wordsworth's) and celebrate nature in its own right.

It is debatable how far critics should base their judgements on what writers choose for their focus, what they include and exclude. For example, how far would we trust a critic who happens to be an ardent Christian and who condemns an otherwise fine novel because it contains no reference to God? Perhaps there is a scale of critic-intervention ranging from the responsible to the absurd? Is there, for example, an essential difference between these two complaints:

- a Marxist critic who deplores Carew's 'Saxham' for flattering its capitalist lord

- an eco-critic attacking Chaucer who, in *The Knight's Tale*, celebrates the funeral pyre for Arcite's death, which felled so many trees and disinherited the animals, birds and the gods of the forest?

Some will argue that it is the critic's job simply to accept the poet's agenda and the cultural assumptions that inform his writing; the critic should concentrate on the poet's rhetorical skills that persuade and give pleasure to readers.

Many modern critics refute this argument as timid and irresponsible. They argue that ecological threat is now so pressing that writers and readers must be constantly aware of it, and that old (unaware) texts must now be read according to our newly responsible principles.

A possible answer to this argument is that ecology is not new: it is older than left-wing / right-wing politics, even older than politics itself. In a disturbed and disoriented world, poetry can take its readers 'home', not in the sense of supplying arguments but through the deeper value of activating the imagination. In his groundbreaking study of Romantic literature *The Song of the Earth* (2000) Jonathan Bate, as an eco-critic, makes an important claim for the primacy of eco-poetics:

> The poet's way of articulating the relationship between human-kind and environment, person and place, is peculiar because it is experiential, not descriptive. Whereas the biologist, the geographer and the Green activist have narratives of dwelling, a poem may be a revelation of dwelling. Such a claim is phenomenological before it is political, and for this reason ecopoetics may be properly regarded as pre-political. Politics, let us remember, means 'of the polis', of the city. For this reason, the controlling myth of ecopoetics is a myth of the pre-political, the prehistoric: it is a Rousseauesque story about imagining a state of nature prior to the fall into property, into inequality and into the city.

Assignments

1 Set up a forum for debate with colleagues about which of these three critical approaches (political, feminist, ecological) is the most helpful in reading literature that includes landscape. What are the values and limitations in reading purely for aesthetic pleasure? It may be helpful to focus this discussion on a single major work: for example, Chaucer's *The Knight's Tale*, Hardy's *Tess of the D'Urbervilles*, Forster's *A Passage to India*.

2 Surveying the literature you know well, compare and contrast the methods of authors who show human beings controlling their landscapes with those who present nature and the land as dominant.

5 | How to write about landscape and literature

- Does landscape description contribute to the work's mood, theme or context?

- When was the piece written? Are there conventions or assumptions behind the author's description of landscape?

- Are there valid ways of reading the piece that have accrued since it was written?

- What are the best ways of organising your responses to the questions above into your own clear and confident writing?

When reading and writing about fictional landscape you need to consider the authors' purposes. In writing about your responses to these books and poems you must beware of criticising them for approaches that they haven't attempted. See, for example, the discussions of the garden of love and Chaucer (see Part 1, page 18 and Part 2, page 40): when reading medieval texts it would often be misguided to look for detailed observation, when the poet is constructing (or even borrowing) an idealised landscape.

In some respects landscape writing makes the same demands as any other type of creative literature: it requires reading that attends to structure, atmosphere, tone and nuances of language; you must listen to the words as well as absorb their surface meaning; in a poem you should try to respond to the form and movement of the verse.

Responding to a poem

This short lyric appears in Tennyson's series of 132 poems known as *In Memoriam*. The poet mourns the premature death of his close friend, Arthur Hallam. Consider the part played by nature and landscape in communicating the poet's grief.

> Old Yew, which graspest at the stones
>   That name the underlying dead,
>   Thy fibres net the dreamless head,
> Thy roots are wrapped about the bones.
>
> The seasons bring the flower again,
>   And bring the firstling to the flock;
>   And in the dusk of thee, the clock
> Beats out the little lives of men.

O not for thee the glow, the bloom,
  Who changest not in any gale,
  Nor branding summer suns avail
To touch thy thousand years of gloom:

And gazing on thee, sullen tree,
  Sick for thy stubborn hardihood,
  I seem to fail from out my blood
And grow incorporate into thee.

The poet is in a graveyard and addresses the yew tree almost throughout the poem. Maybe you find this evasive, but the tree could be seen as an **objective correlative**, a way of focusing the pain on something that is neither the suffering poet nor his dead friend. The tree is dark, impassive, even cruel ('graspest', 'branding', 'beats out'). Note how great age – the yew is the oldest of trees and lives with the dead – outlasts strong human feeling, which later in this lyric is treated almost as a sign of frailty. Look at the tree's relationship with the graveyard bones beneath (not Hallam's): the important words, as so often, are verbs – 'net', 'wrapped about'. What is the relationship here: protection? possession? embrace?

Time may seem static when one contemplates the tree. But time passes in the wider world (stanza 2) – a world very distant from the speaker and the tree. There are 'seasons', lambs being born, blooming flowers, rough gales and hot summer sun. But the churchyard clock is under the tree's authority and it does more than just 'measure' time, which does more than simply 'pass'. The clock 'beats out the little lives of men'. 'Beats out' is a chilling moment of wordplay: it means chime and also assault or destroy. The poet seems to imply that whereas time and the seasons keep renewing the natural world, man's life is 'little' and terminal.

The unchanging tree seems to command the clock, whose relentless time commands our brief time to pass and end. Being vulnerable to time is also what makes us sensitive to feeling – to both joy and grief. If we had the tree's 'stubborn hardihood' we would be immune to any sort of tenderness; the last two lines show the poet seeming to lose what makes him human and 'grow incorporate' into the yew. Is this a wish or an irresistible fascination that appals him? Would it be achievement or failure if he could subdue his capacity to feel? Perhaps there is an ambiguity here, though later in the whole elegy Tennyson writes in a different mood: he will declare firmly that 'Tis better to have loved and lost / Than never to have loved at all.'

Responding to prose

This passage is taken from the opening of 'Odour of Chrysanthemums', a short story by D.H. Lawrence, written in 1910 at the end of the Edwardian era. But, unlike much Edwardian writing, it is not set in a prosperous or privileged part of

England. Lawrence was born in Eastwood, a deprived and ugly mining village near Nottingham, and many of his stories and novels show how people struggle there to maintain life and dignity.

> The small locomotive engine, Number 4, came clanking, stumbling down from Selston with seven full wagons. It appeared round the corner with loud threats of speed, but the colt that it startled from among the gorse, which still flickered indistinctly in the raw afternoon, out-distanced it at a canter. A woman, walking up the railway line to Underwood, drew back into the hedge, held her basket aside, and watched the footplate of the engine advancing. The trucks thumped heavily past, one by one, with slow inevitable movement, as she stood insignificantly trapped between the jolting black wagons and the hedge; then they curved away towards the coppice where the withered oak leaves dropped noiselessly, while the birds, pulling at the scarlet hips beside the track, made off into the dusk that had already crept into the spinney. In the open, the smoke from the engine sank and cleaved to the rough grass. The fields were dreary and forsaken, and in the marshy strip that led to the whimsy, a reedy pit-pond, the fowls had already abandoned their run among the alders, to roost in the tarred fowl-house. The pit-bank loomed up beyond the pond, flames like red sores licking its ashy sides, in the afternoon's stagnant light. Just beyond rose the tapering chimneys and the clumsy black headstocks of Brinsley Colliery. The two wheels were spinning fast up against the sky, and the winding engine rapped out its little spasms. The miners were being turned up.

You should consider the clear structure that Lawrence gives to this passage: the first three brief sentences relate machinery to animal to human life, then the description opens out to the wider context of the landscape. Note the definite article – 'the' – for the engine and the colt, but 'a' woman walking becomes 'insignificantly trapped'. What does this suggest about the relationship between animals at one extreme, whose natural life is disturbed, and powerful industry at the other (while human beings, some of whom are responsible for mechanised 'progress', occupy uneasy territory between)? Note too the words, chiefly verbs, that describe movement: 'stumbling', 'canter', 'walking'. The horse and the birds escape, but the woman has to stand.

See how Lawrence, through the journey of the locomotive, suggests an invasion. In other circumstances the withered oak leaves dropping might evoke simply the natural process of autumn, but here the landscape seems assaulted and occupied. Even when the engine has passed its smoke quietly takes over: it 'cleaved to the rough grass'. 'Cleaved' is an archaic word – does it have a particular effect here? Most of the second half is silent after the sudden noise of the start.

The language suggests desolation ('dreary and forsaken', 'abandoned', 'stagnant') and disease ('red sores', 'little spasms'). What is the effect of the large and heavy words that describe the pit's machinery against the simplicity of Lawrence's final sentence?

Comparison

You will often be asked to compare two passages that describe landscape. There is generally some common ground between them, but then the differences become sharp and interesting. Here are the openings of two late 20th-century novels set in holiday resorts where the combination of land and water attracts the visitors:

> An easterly is the most disagreeable wind in Lyme Bay – Lyme Bay being that largest bite from the underside of England's outstretched south-western leg – and a person of curiosity could at once have deduced several strong probabilities about the pair who began to walk down the quay at Lyme Regis, the small but ancient eponym of the inbite, one incisively sharp and blustery morning in the late March of 1867.
>
> The Cobb has invited what familiarity breeds for at least seven hundred years, and the real Lymers will never see much more to it than a long claw of old grey wall that flexes itself against the sea. In fact, since it lies well apart from the main town, a tiny Piraeus to a microscopic Athens, they seem almost to turn their backs on it. Certainly it has cost them enough in repairs through the centuries to justify a certain resentment. But to a less tax-paying, or more discriminating, eye it is quite simply the most beautiful sea-rampart on the south coast of England. And not only because it is, as the guide-books say, redolent of seven hundred years of English history, because ships sailed to meet the Armada from it, because Monmouth landed beside it ... but finally because it is a superb fragment of folk-art.
>
> Primitive yet complex, elephantine but delicate: as full of subtle curves and volumes as a Henry Moore or a Michelangelo; and pure, clean, salt, a paragon of mass. I exaggerate? Perhaps, but I can be put to the test, for the Cobb has changed very little since the year of which I write; though the town of Lyme has, and the test is not fair if you look backwards towards land.
>
> However, if you had turned northward and landward in 1867, as the man that day did, your prospect would have been harmonious. A picturesque congeries of some dozen or so houses and a small boatyard – in which, arklike on its stocks, sat the thorax of a lugger – huddled at where the Cobb runs back to land. Half a mile to the east lay, across sloping meadows, the thatched and slated roofs of

Lyme itself; a town that had its heyday in the Middle Ages and has been declining ever since. To the west sombre grey cliffs, known locally as Ware Cleeves, rose steeply from the shingled beach where Monmouth entered upon his idiocy. Above them and beyond, stepped massively inland, climbed further cliffs masked by dense woods. It is in this aspect that the Cobb seems most a last bulwark – against all that wild eroding coast to the west. There too I can be put to proof. No house lay visibly then or, beyond a brief misery of beach-huts, lies today in that direction.

(from the opening of *The French Lieutenant's Woman* by John Fowles, 1969)

From the window all that could be seen was a receding area of grey. It was to be supposed that beyond the grey garden, which seemed to sprout nothing but the stiffish leaves of some unfamiliar plant, lay the vast grey lake, spreading like an anaesthetic towards the invisible further shore, and beyond that, in imagination only, yet verified by the brochure, the peak of the Dent d'Oche, on which snow might already be slightly and silently falling. For it was late September, out of season; the tourists had gone, the rates were reduced, and there were few inducements for visitors in this small town at the water's edge, whose inhabitants, uncommunicative to begin with, were frequently rendered taciturn by the dense cloud that descended for days at a time and then vanished without warning to reveal a new landscape, full of colour and incident: boats skimming on the lake, passengers at the landing stage, an open-air market, the outline of the gaunt remains of a thirteenth-century castle, seams of white on the far mountains, and on the cheerful uplands to the south a rising backdrop of apple trees, the fruit sparkling with emblematic significance. For this was a land of prudently harvested plenty, a land which had conquered human accidents, leaving only the weather distressingly beyond control.

(from the opening of *Hotel du Lac* by Anita Brookner, 1984)

These passages are not, like whole poems, complete in themselves. The authors aim to provide a context for the novels' first event or people. In a good novel the descriptions will be more than topographical: they will convey an attitude, atmosphere or tone that suits the author's overall approach. The opening pages will condition the reader's mind towards (for example) calmness, sensation, discomfort, introspection, wit, robust energy. They are written to excite some sort of expectation. Therefore when you write your comparison you are responding to more than mere information.

Consider the novelist's presence in these extracts – lively, often challenging, in the first, and calm almost to extinction, in the second. What about the amount and quality of information? You may think that Fowles has found a guidebook (giving history and topography) and decided to give it an assertive personality. Brookner has one too, but her phrase 'verified by the brochure' is formally restrained.

She remains discreetly behind the window mentioned in her first sentence. Her reflections, as well as what she sees, are coloured by 'grey' (twice in two lines), then by further muted words and phrases: 'anaesthetic', 'seemed to sprout nothing', 'invisible, 'reduced', 'slightly and silently', 'few inducements'. When the dense cloud rises, she brings in some colour and energy but the single sentence simply lists what a lively eye can take in, then settles into the prudent harvest. However, the elegant cadences of that sentence have the control of a well-wrought tapestry. 'Distressingly beyond control' is a telling phrase: it implies that control is crucial, and that adventure or improvisation may be too alarming to contemplate. Or, since this applies to the weather, could the phrase be ironic?

Fowles moves about, physically and mentally: Piraeus, Athens, Michelangelo, Henry Moore, the Armada, the Middle Ages, the Duke of Monmouth. He is 'a person of curiosity' and invites us to be one too. In all this energy how prominent is landscape? Can you picture the scene? Or are you more in touch with the author who views it? It is hard to tell whether he wants us to return to 1867 or to remain where we are with all the advantages of historical comparison. Perhaps you find this uncertainty more exciting than confusing; after all, good stories don't reveal all their secrets at once. On the other hand, there may be a different sort of value in Brookner's elegant and settled approach. A withdrawn personality may have its depths that are worth encountering.

When you have gathered your thoughts about the passages and begin to think about organising them into paragraphs, remember that the question asks you to *compare* the two openings. You can't easily do this if you just divide your answer into two parts – one for Fowles, one for Brookner. Try instead to devote each paragraph to a single aspect or area of interest; then within the paragraph consider both writers and establish points of comparison and contrast. It is unlikely that every paragraph can work in this way, but if most do, you will persuade your reader that your essay is a genuine comparison.

Preparing to write about a topic

Suppose you are studying literature about Englishness and your topic is to *explore how landscape interacts with a sense of social class*. Within the last 120 years a rich variety of novels and poems (and a few plays) appears in this category. Here are just a few of the many that are worth considering:

A.E. Housman *A Shropshire Lad*
E.M. Forster *Howards End*
Evelyn Waugh *Brideshead Revisited*
John Betjeman's poems

D.H. Lawrence *The Rainbow* and *Women in Love*
L.P. Hartley *The Go-Between*
Kazuo Ishiguro *The Remains of the Day*
Tom Stoppard *Arcadia*
Poems by Edward Thomas and many of the Georgian poets

Your reading may also take you back to some regional novels of the Victorian age
or into the 18th century, especially books that celebrate the country house and the
landed gentry. Very little of what you read will be wholly about landscape, but where
it does appear it has significant effects on how you respond to the events, people
and attitudes.

You cannot cover it all, and if you aim to touch on too many books you will
become a sort of butterfly critic, briefly alighting to make a mention, then flying off
restlessly to another book. It is better to decide on a few major works about which
you feel well-informed and confident, and then use these for sections of close
critical analysis. The others, which hold minor importance in your essay, may be
used for comparison, contrast and brief allusion.

Literature branches out into the other arts; depending on your interests, you
may find relevant stimulus in music, painting or film. Two great composers, Elgar
(1857–1934) and Vaughan Williams (1872–1958), are associated with Englishness,
some of their works evoking specific landscapes. Gainsborough (1727–1788),
Constable (1776–1837) and Turner (1775–1851) were all landscape artists; many
of their works are on display in The National Gallery and Tate Britain. More
recent artists are Eric Ravilious (1903–1942), with his celebrated watercolours of
the English landscape, and John Piper (1903–1992) who was influenced by the
imminent devastation of the Second World War to create topographical records of
many English churches in their landscapes.

Several critics and commentators have tried to capture the essence of
Englishness. In 1955 Nikolaus Pevsner gave a series of Reith lectures on BBC
radio which he later turned into *The Englishness of English Art*. Being foreign
(a German refugee from Hitler's regime) he brings a helpful objectivity to his study.
Roy Strong's *The Spirit of Britain*, subtitled 'A Narrative History of the Arts', relates
the arts to each other and to developments in history.

A word of warning about this topic. Many of the authors (more so than the
commentators) are conservative and nostalgic. Nostalgia helps to explain the
popularity of some middlebrow TV crime-stories, such as Agatha Christie's Miss
Marple series or *Midsomer Murders*. Much English literature is given a rural
setting, which often conveys reassuring establishment values; note how many
of the famous public schools were built in the country and how major political
decisions have often been made at statesmen's country houses. The popularity
of Trollope's and Austen's novels has much to do with their setting. This positive

attitude to country life is far more English than European: Chekhov's *Three Sisters*, for example, and Flaubert's *Madame Bovary* show women bored to distraction by rural stillness and longing for the vibrant cities.

You need to be aware that objective, even hostile, readings of Englishness are possible and valid. Marxist and feminist critics (see Part 4, pages 104 and 105) are often stringent and attack class and gender-based notions of what is traditionally English.

George Orwell's essay 'The Lion and the Unicorn' was written in 1941 when England was in the middle of a devastating war, and moves from the English character, as he sees it, to views on foreign policy and socialist ideals. Jeremy Paxman's *The English* (1999) and Roger Scruton's *England: an Elegy* (2000) both cover wide-ranging aspects of the English character. They speculate on how the English came to have an idyllic view of their past, closely identified with rural charm: 'the land of lost content' and 'those blue remembered hills', as Housman put it in *A Shropshire Lad*. Orwell believed that 'England is the most class-ridden country under the sun. It is a land of snobbery and privilege, ruled largely by the old and silly.'

Writing about the topic

Try to plan your essay into sections, each of which deals with an aspect of the larger topic but which also connects logically with what comes before and after. Some sections may be devoted to close analysis but several should include comparison and allusion. Consider the interests of your reader. You should aim to convey not just information and opinion but also a lively and committed approach; you can go some way to achieving this if your overall method moves between close scrutiny and a broader treatment.

The first section allows you different possible approaches. A safe and clear method would be to define the parameters of your treatment (for example, in historical period or range of opinion) and to indicate the line of thought you intend to take. But you may instead take your cue from quality journalism where authors begin their features with something specific – in this case, perhaps a letter, review, anecdote, quotation or unusual fact, which may give some life and individuality and surprise your reader into brisk attention. For this topic on how landscape interacts with social class you could begin with a nostalgic verse from one of the Georgian poets, or a sharp sentence of criticism from Orwell, Scruton or Paxman, or some lines from Pope that declare principles for landscape gardening. Whatever you choose, you must show its relevance by how you reflect on it immediately afterwards, and then by how you move into your next section.

The main business of your writing should become established in the more substantial *second section*. Here are some possibilities for this and for *what follows*.

In *The Go-Between* there are three social groups: Lord Trimingham, who owns Brandham Hall; the upper middle-class Maudesleys, who live there; Ted Burgess, the tenant-farmer on Trimingham's land, living in his cottage. The 'green' (in other words, naive) little boy, Leo Colston, observes and partly tells their stories through his own. Much depends on a combination of hot weather and landscape. You might focus on scenes like the swimming party, Leo's journeys from hall to farm, the out-houses, the symbolic value of scenery at the cricket match – and the way the landscape and Brandham Hall appear when he returns as an older man.

In Evelyn Waugh's *Brideshead Revisited* a great house and its grounds also contain a seductive style of life and an outsider / narrator who responds and judges – and returns with his memories. Charles Ryder, an aspiring artist, makes a painting of the house in its landscape. His view as a young romantic, coloured by his sybaritic life at Oxford, contrasts with the grim effects of wartime on the house, which frame the almost fantasy-life of the whole story. Landscape and history interact to make readers reflect on changing times, however much they and the characters wish to preserve the status quo.

In *Howards End* E.M. Forster is more elusive about the spirit of the house but more convinced that it must be preserved (see Part 4, page 106). But he often adopts an arch, even sly, tone and undermines what also attracts him about characters and places. You might examine his imagined tourist's view of England (opening of Chapter 19: 'If one wanted to show a foreigner England …') and the woodcutter's view of Mrs Wilcox's funeral (Chapter 11). Forster has been often criticised for his depiction of the poor and uneducated in their environments; in general, his sympathies are limited to certain types of middle-class life.

But not everyone in the country enjoys a privileged life. Lawrence, for example, pays much attention to the contrast between social deprivation and intense primal feelings. He also contrasts the fecundity of the earth with harsh industrial towns and also with the debilitation that can occur when someone is educated away from the land and towards middle-class delicacy. Look, for example, at the extract from *The Rainbow* (see Part 3, page 95) and in Chapter 16 at Ursula's journey, with the rain, the wood and the horses. In his short story 'The Man who Loved Islands' he satirises a fastidious man who is destroyed by his isolation; Lawrence achieves much of his effect here by ironic appreciation of landscape beauty. In *Cold Comfort Farm* (see Part 3, page 97) Stella Gibbons writes an amusing and mischievous parody of Lawrence at his most intense.

Seen from another point of view, the ordinary countryman, often known generically as 'Hodge', may appear merely dogged and devoid of personality. But this emptiness may be a defence against feeling how powerless he is; decisions are made for him, as with the young drummer boy in Hardy's poem 'Drummer Hodge' who is sent to the Boer War and dies in an alien landscape. Housman's *A Shropshire Lad* (1896) begins with calls for the generic 'lad' to enlist, and ends with lyrics of premature death and lost youth. The rhyming quatrains have the quality of an elegiac ballad, a melancholy charm evoking the landscape of the border country around Ludlow. Housman conveys scenery chiefly through flowers, place-names ('By Ony and Teme and Clun') and the music of his verse.

Some critics will find it patronising for a highly educated classical scholar like Housman to look down from his ivory tower on the lad from Shropshire. Raymond Williams (see Part 4, page 105) was irritated when Edward Thomas, one of the prominent Georgian poets, condensed all of history into 'Lob', the irrepressible countryman who has seen and endured everything. With colloquial energy Thomas implies that in him the spirit of England remains close to the earth:

> The man was wild
> And wandered. His home was where he was free.
> Everybody has met one such man as he.

Housman and Thomas are popular because they are easy to read – easy to criticise too, especially as they seem old-fashioned, lacking grit or experiment, and writing as the modernist movement was beginning.

When you write you should focus and analyse far more than has been possible in this brief survey. There is also much scope for cross-reference. For example: regional comparisons and differences; symbolic or allegorical landscapes; treatments of houses, gardens and churches; whether the landscapes contribute to substance or merely to charm; degrees of mockery, irony or more serious undermining.

Assignments

1   Select two or three novels or stories which open with landscape description and consider how the contexts of place, mood and tone are made appropriate to the people and events which follow. You could make a similar comparison between the openings of novels by George Eliot and John Steinbeck (see Part 3, pages 93 and 94).

2   Using advice given in the section on 'Writing about the topic' (see page 117, above), plan your own extended essay on *Landscapes for fantasy writing* or *Landscapes for love stories* or *Landscapes of war*.

3   Compare and contrast the work of any two landscape artists (several are mentioned on page 116, above). Do you find that their priorities are to record or to invent or to persuade viewers to accept a social or political agenda?

6 | Resources

Further reading

Malcolm Andrews *Landscape and Western Art* (*Oxford History of Art* series, Oxford University Press, 1999)
Focuses on the visual arts (but alludes to literature). Helpful surveys of topography, the picturesque and the sublime – and theories of landscape, both political and philosophical.

John Barrell and John Bull, ed. *The Penguin Book of Pastoral Verse* (Penguin, 1984)

John Barrell *The Idea of Landscape and the Sense of Place* (Cambridge University Press, 1972)
An examination of 18th-century landscape literature and the impact of the picturesque, followed by the effects of agricultural improvement. The book's second half and real focus is the sense of unique place in Clare's poetry.

Jonathan Bate *The Song of the Earth* (Picador, 2000)
About alienation from nature and how poetry (chiefly Romantic) can restore us to a deeper sense of dwelling on the earth.

Jonathan Bate *Romantic Ecology: Wordsworth and the Environmental Tradition* (Routledge, 1991)
Examines Wordsworth's poetry and John Ruskin's theories of nature to develop a 'green' approach to criticism of the Romantics, and challenges utilitarian and Marxist interpretations.

A.S. Byatt *Unruly Times* (1970; Vintage, 1997)
A study of the literary partnership of Wordsworth and Coleridge in a lively social and political era. It includes a succinct and informative chapter on landscape.

Collette Clark, ed. *Home at Grasmere* (Penguin, 1978)
Selected extracts from the journal of Dorothy Wordsworth, many of them related to poems by her brother William.

Michael Ferber *Dictionary of Literary Symbols* (Cambridge University Press, 2007)
Lists references from the natural world used in English literature and gives very full accounts of their symbolic meanings.

Greg Garrard *Ecocriticism* (*The New Critical Idiom* series, Routledge, 2004)
Explores the ways in which we imagine and portray the relationship between humans and the environment in all areas of cultural production.

Ken Hiltner *Milton and Ecology* (Cambridge University Press, 2003)
Argues that Milton's use of nature anticipates 20th-century theories of ecology.
Pays particular attention to *Paradise Lost*.

Frank Kermode *English Pastoral Poetry* (Harrap, 1952)
An anthology of pastoral poems from the early Middle Ages to Marvell, with a
helpful introduction on the classical origins of pastoral.

Carolyn Merchant *The Death of Nature: Women, Ecology and the Scientific
Revolution* (Harper Collins, 1980)
A feminist and historical approach to the subject.

James Sambrook *English Pastoral Poetry* (Twayne, 1983)
A clear account of the development of pastoral poetry through Spenser, Sidney,
Milton, Marvell, Pope and Wordsworth, as well as lesser known poets.

Simon Schama *Landscape and Memory* (Harper Collins, 1995)
A vast, learned and lively study of our relationship with the landscape, engaging
with myth, history and the arts.

Martin Wiener *English Culture and the Decline of the Industrial Spirit 1850–1980*
(Cambridge University Press, 1983)
A social and political study of attitudes to change and stability in city and country.

Raymond Williams *The Country and the City* (1973; Hogarth, 1993)
The author takes a Marxist approach to the contrast of country and city.

Media resources: film and television

When watching films or television series of books you should make important
judgements: are they to be enjoyed as independent productions, or as helpful
re-creations of the book? You may judge that reading a book is such a different
activity from watching a film that the one can never replicate the other. This may
raise a particular question with landscape: a writer is likely to be selective (and
sometimes symbolic) in what he or she asks you to 'see', whereas many films are
more spectacular and comprehensive. You may feel that some films or series depart
so far from the spirit and details of the book that they should be advertised as being
'loosely based on the plot of …'.

However, there are several excellent films and television series made from some
of the novels discussed in this book:

Jane Austen *Pride and Prejudice* (Simon Langton for BBC TV, 1995; Joe Wright,
2005)
Jane Austen *Sense and Sensibility* (Ang Lee, 1995; John Alexander for BBC TV,
2008)

E.M. Forster *Howards End* (Merchant / Ivory, 1992)

Thomas Hardy *Tess of the D'Urbervilles* (Roman Polanski, 1980; David Blair for BBC TV, 2008)

Thomas Hardy *Far from the Madding Crowd* (John Schlesinger, 1967)

Thomas Hardy *The Mayor of Casterbridge* (David Giles, 1978; David Thacker, 2003; both for BBC TV)

L.P. Hartley *The Go-Between* (Joseph Losey, 1970)

Ian McEwan *Atonement* (Joe Wright, 2007)

Evelyn Waugh *Brideshead Revisited* (Charles Sturridge for ITV, 1981; Julian Jarrold, 2008)

Websites

There has often been a close relationship between literature and the visual arts. You can access works by, for example, Claude, Poussin, Watteau, Gainsborough, Constable, Joseph Wright, Turner, Nash, Piper, Ravilious on the Internet. Useful sites are:

www.all-art.org/contents.html
www.wga.hu
www.artcyclopedia.com

Glossary

Allegory an extended metaphor in which a story or description carries a half-hidden meaning, usually moral or religious. It therefore works on two related levels, as with Spenser's *The Faerie Queen* and Bunyan's *A Pilgrim's Progress*.

Conceit in its literary sense, a 'conceit' is a witty, ingenious and surprising comparison, often found in metaphysical poetry of the early 17th century.

Decorum appropriateness. 'Decorum' in literature means that the writer chooses the appropriate style of writing to suit the subject matter.

Enlightenment the word refers to the light of reason and is applied to philosophy and art in the 18th century, based on the development of scientific thought to explain the world and to ensure human progress towards perfection. Enlightenment thinkers dismissed superstition and were often sceptical about religion.

Epigram a succinct piece of writing with a witty turn of phrase.

Fin amour or 'courtly love' (as it became known in the 19th century). A knight's dedication to his lady, as idealised in early medieval French literature and Chaucer's 14th-century contemporaries.

Georgian poets the group of largely pastoral and lyric poets known as the Georgians (after George V who reigned from 1910 to 1936).

Heroic couplet two lines in rhyming iambic pentameter used in 17th-century heroic verse tragedies. It was then widely used for many poetic genres in the 18th century.

Iconography the conventional imagery associated with a subject, especially religious.

Locus amoenus literally ' a pleasant place' or (more idealistically) the garden of beauty and delight, which is the traditional setting for many medieval stories of *fin amour*. From *amoenus* comes our word 'amenity'.

Myth a story, carrying spiritual significance, that explains the origin of natural phenomena. A myth is often part of traditional folklore (before recorded history) and generally includes gods or heroes.

Neo-Platonism Plotinus and other 3rd-century philosophers were later described as 'neo' (new) Platonists because their support for Plato's beliefs was refined and developed. Versions of neo-Platonism (especially in theories of the human soul) also appeared among Renaissance thinkers.

Objective correlative term coined by T.S. Eliot in his essay on *Hamlet* (1919). He believed that the only way to express emotion is often to find 'a set of objects, a situation, a chain of events which shall be the formula of that *particular* emotion'.

Pantheism a belief that God exists in everything.

Pathetic fallacy the phrase derives from an error (fallacy) and feeling (pathos) and denotes the practice of pretending that nature can feel human emotions, generally to emphasise the same emotions felt by characters in the story or poem. The phrase was coined by John Ruskin in *Modern Painters* (1846).

Persona a fictitious character, appearing as the first-person 'I' to tell the story in a poem or novel.

Pre-lapsarian before the Fall of Man. The word refers to the state of Adam and Eve in the Garden of Eden before their sin of disobedience.

Pre-Raphaelite in 1848 a group of artists, writers and critics set out to revive the principles of art and craftsmanship that had flourished in the late Middle Ages (before Raphael). Artists such as Millais, Rossetti, Morris and Holman Hunt were notable for their highly detailed studies of nature, for high moral intentions and much religious and mystical work. The critic John Ruskin became their most fervent spokesman and opponent of all that was shoddy and ugly in contemporary life and art.

Renaissance literally a 'rebirth' of intellectual and artistic life. It is impossible to date the Renaissance period exactly, but it spread from Italy (especially Florence) throughout Europe between 1400 and 1650. It included the rediscovery of classical learning, the development of science and the growth of patronage of the arts by noble families.

Rhetoric the art of persuasion through language, and an important branch of ancient and Renaissance education. In modern times 'rhetoric' has become a negative label for pretentious and empty language, especially when used by politicians.

Romantic partly a reaction against the formal, classical, rationalistic attitudes that had dominated European arts and literature during the 18th century. Romanticism stressed the importance of the imagination, of the emotional and the irrational; it privileged the individual (especially the outsider) over society.

Tabula rasa from Latin for 'a blank slate', it refers to the theory that the personality is empty until sensory and intellectual knowledge is 'written' upon it from the experiences of life.

Topographical writing which focuses on a particular place, giving precise descriptions and often incidental meditation. Many 18th-century topographical poems praise country houses and their estates.

Topos literally (from the Greek) 'a place', it came to mean any standard theme or topic (such as the great flood or deluge) that became the basis for many literary treatments. The garden of love is a recurrent *topos* in medieval literature.

Vernacular the native language of a place or country. For example, much early medieval writing in England was in Latin or French (especially for administration, the law and the Church); eventually the English vernacular was more widely used.

Index

Actaeon 15
Addison, Joseph 27–8
allegory 11–12, 19, 23, 52, 122
Andrews, Malcolm 29, 52
anti-pastoral 23–4
Antony, Mark 12, 13
Armitage, Simon 79, 84–5
Arnold, Matthew 49, 61, 92–3
art 7, 8–9, 26, 52
Augustan poetry 13, 35
Augustus (Octavian) 12, 13, 14–15
Austen, Jane 30, 36, 37, 57–8, 59, 90–1

Barrell, John 72
Bate, Jonathan 72, 105, 107, 109
beautiful 30, 65
Beckett, Samuel 43
Beckford, William 35
Bible 7, 15–16, 16–17, 25, 26, 42
Blake, William 34
Blunden, Edmund 78, 96–7
Brontë, Charlotte 35, 37, 66
Brontë, Emily 35, 37, 59–60, 66
Brooke, Rupert 52
Brookner, Anita 114–15
Brown, Lancelot Capability 27
Bunyan, John 52
Burke, Edmund 33–4, 65, 66

Carew, Thomas 57, 86
Carson, Rachel 76–7
Carter, Angela 35, 100–1
Chaucer, Geoffrey Book of the Duchess
    50; from Canterbury Tales 21, 41–3;
    'Parlement of Foulys' 18–19, 85, 105
childhood 62–5
Clare, John 33, 36–7, 62, 72, 86–7, 107
classical influences 11–15, 25, 78–82
Claude Lorrain 28–9
Coleridge, Samuel Taylor 32–5, 61, 63–4,
    65–6
Collins, Wilkie 35
comparisons 113–15
conceit 23, 48, 122
Conrad, Joseph 77
Constable, John 104, 116
country house poems 56–61

Crabbe, George 104
Craig, Edward Gordon 43

Daphne 14
Darwin, Charles 32, 69
decorum 12, 50, 122
deep ecology 32, 108
desolation 76–8
Dickens, Charles 35, 37–8
Donne, John 24, 42
Drayton, Michael 23
dream poetry 18–19, 50

ecology 76, 105, 106–7
Eden 12, 15–17, 23–4, 41–2, 47, 49, 52–3
elegy 49–52, 119
Elgar, Edward 116
Eliot, George 21, 37, 62–3, 75, 93–4
Eliot, T.S. 55–6, 98–9
emblem books 26
enclosure acts 33, 36–7
England's Helicon 23
Englishness 116, 117
Enlightenment 26–31, 34–5, 58, 64, 122
epigrams 11, 122
essay-planning 117–19
Evelyn, John 53

feminist criticism 105–6, 117
feudalism 103
fin amour 17, 19, 42, 123
forest 20, 50, 53
Forster, E.M. 106, 118
Fowles, John 113–15

Gainsborough, Thomas 116
gardens 17–20, 41–2, 110; see also Eden
Gaskell, Elizabeth 37
Genesis 15–16
genius of the place 27, 58
Georgian poetry 105, 119, 123
Gibbons, Stella 97–8, 118
Gilpin, William 28, 29–31, 30–1, 33, 66
Golding, William 65, 99–100
Goldsmith, Oliver 77–8, 104
gothic 30, 33, 34–5, 65, 66–7
Gray, Thomas 51

Hardy, Thomas 37; *Far from the Madding Crowd* 21, 67–8, 70; *Mayor of Casterbridge* 69; poems 13, 51, 52, 68–9, 118; *Return of the Native* 68, 69; *Tess of the D'Urbervilles* 21, 69
Hartley, L.P. 59, 118
Heaney, Seamus 51, 79, 80–2, 105
heroic couplets 57, 123
Hood, Robin 20, 21
Hopkins, Gerard Manley 49, 53, 54, 71, 87
Housman, A.E. 51, 117, 118–19
Hughes, Ted 15, 79, 80, 101–2
hunting 21, 45

iconography 42, 43, 123
idylls 21–2
inscape/instress 54, 71
intuition 27, 70
Isaiah 26

Jacobean tragedy 35
Johnson, Samuel 50–1
Jonson, Ben 56–7

Keats, John 6, 26, 50, 73, 74, 76–7
Kent, William 27

Lake District 31, 33
land 8–9, 73–4, 76–7
landscape 7, 8–9; childhood 62–5; desolation 76–8; in films 59; moral/social 57–8; nostalgia 28; politics 103–5, 109; religion 52–6; sublime 33; women 69–70
landscape gardening 26, 27
Lawrence, D.H. 95–6, 111–13, 118
Lewis, Matthew 35
locus amoenus 17, 42, 123
de Lorris, Guillaume 19

McEwan, Ian 59
Marlowe, Christopher 24
Marvell, Andrew 46–9
Marxist criticism 104–5, 117
mechanisation 112–13
memory 24, 25–6, 63
Merchant, Carolyn 105
Meun, Jean de 19
Millais, John 75–6
Milton, John 8; *Lycidas* 50–1; *Paradise Lost* 8, 16, 34, 52–3, 88, 107

Murdoch, Iris 35
myths 14, 15–16, 123

nature 7, 9; art 26; deep ecology 108; and God 105; grief 110–11; politics 45–6; productivity 56–7; Shakespeare 43–6; symbolism 24–6
neo-platonism 105, 123
nostalgia 6, 11, 28, 61, 63, 103, 116–17

objective correlative 111, 123
Octavian, *see* Augustus
Orpheus 15
Orwell, George 117
Ovid 14–15, 26, 44, 47

pantheism 61, 123
pastoral poetry 7, 8, 11, 44, 48–9, 103
pastoralism 6, 21–2, 23, 107
pathetic fallacy 12, 123
Paxman, Jeremy 117
persona 18, 123
Pevsner, Nikolaus 116
picturesque 27, 29–31, 58, 90–1
Piper, John 116
Plato 47, 105
Poe, Edgar Allen 35
politics 45–6, 103–5, 109
Pope, Alexander 13, 27, 28, 35, 57
prelapsarian state 23–4, 123
pre-Raphaelites 75–6, 124
Proserpina 14
Psalms 25
Puttenham, George 23

Quennell, Peter 64

Radcliffe, Ann 35
Raleigh, Walter 24
Ravilious, Eric 116
religion 52–6
Renaissance 16, 21–2, 26, 49, 52, 124
rhetoric 34, 124
Roman de la Rose 17, 18–20, 41
Romantics 31–3, 60–2, 65, 66–7, 124
Rosa, Salvator 65–6
Rosenberg, Isaac 26
Rousseau, Jean Jacques 31–3, 38, 64
Ruskin, John 29

Schama, Simon 20
Scruton, Roger 117
Shakespeare, William 43–6; *Hamlet*
    24–5; *Henry V* 45–6; *King Lear* 44;
    Love's Labours Lost 22; *Midsummer*
    Night's Dream 15, 43; *Othello* 25;
    Pericles 44; *Richard II* 26, 45–6;
    Tempest 15, 44; *Two Gentlemen of*
    Verona 20; *Winter's Tale* 44; *As You*
    Like It 20, 21, 24, 45
Shelley, Mary 67
Shelley, Percy Bysshe 33, 91–2
Sidney, Philip 22–3, 56
Sir Gawain and the Green Knight 21, 79,
    84–5
social divisions 104, 115–17
solitude 7
Song of Solomon 16–17, 42
Sparta 32
Spenser, Edmund 11, 22
Steinbeck, John 94–5
Stoker, Bram 35
Stoppard, Tom 58
Strong, Roy 116
sublime 30–1, 33–4, 65, 66–7
symbolism 24–6, 65, 110–11

tabula rasa 18, 124
taste 27, 30, 31, 34–5, 58
Taylor, John 72
Tennyson, Alfred 11, 110–11
Thelwall, John 65
Theocritus 11, 22

Thomas, Dylan 64–5
Thomas, Edward 105, 108, 119
Thomas, R.S. 74
Thomson, James 88–9
Thoreau, Henry David 38–9, 82, 107
time passing 24–5, 65, 111
topography 43, 69, 124
topos 40, 124
tourism 28, 30, 31
Traherne, Thomas 64
Tree, Beerbohm 43
Trollope, Anthony 37
Turner, William 65–6, 116

Vaughan Williams, Ralph 116
Vayghan, Henry 64
vernacular 22, 124
Virgil 11, 12–13, 22, 26, 28, 52, 74
Walpole, Horace 35
water/time symbolism 24–5, 65
Waugh, Evelyn 24, 118
Webster, John 35
Wilbur, Richard 74
Williams, Raymond 105, 119
Wordsworth, Dorothy 70–1, 89–90
Wordsworth, William on childhood
    62, 63–4; *Guide to the Lakes* 31;
    'Intimations of Immortality' 64, 65,
    66; *Lyrical Ballads* 33, 63–4, 73–4,
    104; 'Michael' 73–4; politics 32, 33;
    Prelude 63; 'Ruined Cottage' 51;
    'Solitary Reaper' 60; and Thoreau 38;
    'Tintern Abbey' 33–4, 60, 70–1

Acknowledgements

The authors and publishers acknowledge the following sources of copyright material and are grateful for the permissions granted. While every effort has been made, it has not always been possible to identify the sources of all the material used, or to trace all copyright holders. If any omissions are brought to our notice, we will be happy to include the appropriate acknowledgements on reprinting.

pp.113–114: Alexander Associates on behalf of the author for an extract from John Fowles *The French Lieutenant's Woman* (1969), Vintage Classics (2004) p.9; pp.72, 86–87, 97–98, 107: Curtis Brown Group Ltd, London on behalf of the Estate of the author for an extract from Stella Gibbons *Cold Comfort Farm* (1932) p.28. Copyright © Stella Gibbons 1932; and on behalf of the translator for John Clare 'Emmonsails Heath in Winter' and extracts from John Clare 'The Shepherd's Calendar' and 'The Flitting', translated by Eric Robinson. Copyright © Eric Robinson 1984; pp.74, 80–81, 82, 84–85, 98–99, 99–100, 101–102: Faber and Faber Ltd and Houghton Mifflin Harcourt Publishing Company for Richard Wilbur 'He Was' from *Ceremony and Other Poems*. Copyright © 1950, renewed 1978 by Richard Wilbur, and for extracts from William Golding *Free Fall* (1959) p. 44. Copyright © 1959 by William Golding, renewed 1987 by W. Gerald Golding and T.S. Eliot 'Little Gidding' from *Four Quartets* by T.S. Eliot. Copyright © 1942 by T.S. Eliot, renewed 1970 by Esme Valerie Eliot; and with WW Norton & Company, Inc for an extract from Simon Armitage, translator, *Sir Gawain and the Green Knight: A New Verse Translation*, p. 29. Copyright © 2007 by Simon Armitage and Seamus Heaney, translator, *Beowulf*. Copyright © 2000 Seamus Heaney; and with Farrar, Straus and Giroux, LLC for Seamus Heaney 'Glanmore Sonnet' from *New Selected Poems* by Seamus Heaney (1990) Faber and Faber and Opened Ground: *Selected Poems 1966–1996* (1998) Farrar Straus and Giroux, LLC. Copyright © 1998 by Seamus Heaney, and an extract from Ted Hughes *Tales From Ovid* (1997) p.128. Copyright © 1997 by Ted Hughes; pp.96–97: PDF on behalf of the Estate of the author for an extract from Edmund Blunden *Undertones of War*, Richard Cobden-Sanderson (1928), Penguin Classics (2000) p.97. Copyright © Edmund Blunden 1928; pp.100–101: Rogers, Coleridge & White Ltd on behalf of the author for an extract from Angela Carter 'The Erl King' from *The Bloody Chamber* by Angela Carter, Vintage (1995) p.84. Copyright © 1979 Angela Carter; p.74: Gwydion Thomas for an extract from R.S. Thomas 'A Muck Farmer'. Copyright © Kunjana Thomas 2001